bonsai landscapes

PETER ADAMS

PHOTOGRAPHS BY BILL JORDAN

WARD LOCK

This book is dedicated to Kate and our children.

A WARD LOCK BOOK

First published in the UK 1999 by Ward Lock
Wellington House, 125 Strand
London WC2R 0BB
www.cassell.co.uk

A Cassell Imprint

Distributed in the United States by
Sterling Publishing Co., Inc.
387 Park Avenue South
New York NY 10016-8810

British Library Cataloguing-in-Publication Data
A catalogue record for this book is available from the British Library

ISBN 0-7063-7767-2

Designed by Richard Carr
Edited by Sarah Widdicombe
Colour separation by Tenon & Polert Colour Scanning Ltd.
Printed and bound by Colorcraft Ltd, Hong Kong

contents

Preface   5

1   Looking at Miniature Landscapes   7

2   Tools and Materials   36

3   Choosing the Plants   40

4   Shaping the Plants   52

5   Making the Landscape   72

6   Making a Rock Planter   82

7   Creating Miniature Landscapes   88

    Tree Care Directory   114

    Glossary   126

    Index   127

Accent plant: The image of the Rocky Mountain juniper would be very austere if unrelieved by the saxifrage accent planting which softens the mood to that of an alpine meadow. (Pacific Rim Bonsai Collection)

preface

Bonsai Landscapes is designed to help you make miniature editions of your favourite landscapes. Using ordinary materials, a plan and a little preparation, your concept can be thought of as part layout and part assembly, and is easily achieved. The book shows you how, and takes you from humble beginnings, through evolving plantings and then to more finished designs, always explaining clearly just how each was created.

What I have done is to combine the bonsai landscape (also known as saikei, a Japanese simulated natural scene) with the bonsai group – and fabulous the mix can be. Some examples will be more landscape than group, and some will turn out closer to the group, but with both the important thing is just to look at the possibilities and have fun! Sometimes it is necessary to allow a little preparation period in which to pre-work the plants so that they meet the requirements of size and shape. Other than that, the time taken to assemble even a fairly elaborate planting is seldom more than a couple of (very enjoyable) hours.

The book starts with a look at some wonderful examples of bonsai landscapes and explains their history and development. From there, practical matters are discussed one by one: tools and materials; suitable plants, where to find them and how to shape them; assembly of a landscape; and how to make a realistic rock planter to hold a tree or even a whole landscape. This practical knowledge is then put to work in the projects section, which gives step-by-step instructions for re-creating the superb landscapes featured in the book. Finally, a comprehensive directory gives full details of how to care for the various tree species throughout the year.

In order to provide an informative mix of photographs, drawings and text, Bill Jordan travelled to the US so that we could work as a production team, and his stunning pictures of a fascinating range of species are the result.

I would like to thank Charlie and Ruth Anderson, Genieve and Jack Enwright, and Ian Stewardson for their invaluable help in allowing me to work with their trees; and David DeGroot, Curator of the Pacific Rim Collection, for allowing us to photograph the saikei and 'Catlin' elm slab planting from the collection. My thanks go also to my old friend Dan Barton, for generously sharing with us all the images of his lovely accent plants in the pots that he, his wife Cecilia and daughter Phyllipa have fashioned so beautifully. Thanks again to my dear wife Kate for her help and unfailing support on a practical level and as production co-ordinator, and to our old friend Bill Jordan for all the time, help and travelling he has put into the project, and of course for the wonderful pictures he has once again created.

I do hope you will enjoy reading the book and making your own miniature bonsai landscapes.

Peter Adams
Port Orchard, Washington

looking at miniature landscapes

This first chapter looks at a number of designs for miniature bonsai landscapes that you can easily adapt for yourself. Think of them as exercises to get your own creative juices flowing, and borrow and learn.

Where possible, I have looked at the landscape before and after a typical refining session, and tried to include a little history. There then follows a discussion of possible evolution for the planting in future years.

CREATING THE EFFECT

The small size of the landscapes we are aiming to create means that the effect produced will be an 'impression' rather than a detailed rendering of a scene, but even so they are very telling. In bonsai, a series of visual tricks is used to suggest extra space: some of the illusions follow the basic rules of perspective, while others use the Japanese principle of 'implied space'.

Groups are usually arranged so that the biggest, thickest trunks are planted in the foreground, with the smallest, thinnest trunks to the rear – this immediately creates distance through perspective. The same group will be planted slightly offset from centre in the pot or to one side, so that the

unoccupied zone suggests space extending into the distance – the Japanese principle of implied space mentioned above.

Texture is a major component in the range of visual tools used by the miniature landscape grower. For example, fine-textured plants may be placed anywhere, but can be used effectively to suggest background and distance. This is particularly convincing if larger-leaved plants appear in the foreground.

The same applies to the choice of rocks and stones. Fabulous effects are possible where the texture of the rocks is carefully considered, so that the various colours, sizes and textures are linked in character but varied in appearance, right down to the choice of the finest sands.

THE LANDSCAPES

The miniature bonsai landscapes described in the following pages vary from those that are evolving to maturing landscapes that have had up to 100 years of care! They have been chosen to demonstrate the special effects made possible through the use of perspective, texture and space. In Chapter 7, full step-by-step instructions are given for re-creating the landscapes yourself.

chinese juniper

SEVEN-TRUNK RAFT ON IBIGAWA ROCK

This planting was put together at a bonsai convention in Portland by Masahiro Furakawa.

Height of rock: 60cm (24in)
Height of juniper: 67.5cm (27in)
Age: 15 years
Size of container: 52.5 x 37.5 x 6.25cm (21 x 15 x 2½in)
Colour of container: grey/brown unglazed

The original concept is interesting and shows a lot of imagination. The technique of applying a raft to a vertical stone sounds very complex but is really quite straightforward and is definitely worth trying, even for the novice.

The first step in a landscape of this type is to consider the rock and work out how to exploit its best features: it is

Chinese juniper: seven-trunk raft on ibigawa rock.

After styling.

growth follows the flow of the rock and visually extends its lines beyond the natural confines of the stone. The downswept foliage profiles echo and counterbalance the visual movement that is created by the standing posture of the rock.

I have drawn an equal weight of foliage on both sides, but as the dynamics of the stone go to the right, I have stabilized the design by placing the highest foliage point over the centre of the rock, so that the centre of gravity passes down through the middle. I still had fun placing the branch lines so that the eye is led from side to side! The foliage canopy swings down closer to the curve of the rock on the left and flows away to the right, making an interesting negative line with the concavity of the rock to the lower right. As the branches are trimmed, underlines will be revealed and hinted at, which adds a lot to the feeling of age.

It is important also to preserve the negative areas in the design. Even when these are just minor indentations that cause shadows, they are significant in making the sweep of the foliage interesting and lively. A problem with Chinese juniper is that it responds so well to soft pinching that trained lines readily become blurred by new foliage, so it does need regular grooming to restore the fine details.

I have added some plant material on the left: dwarf grasses would work well. The container has been changed for a shallower oval, and a dull blue would be pleasing.

important not to cover up too much of it. In this example, the artist made clever use of the vertical character of the rock and its natural protrusions, so that when planted the whole would resemble an old trunk with jutting branches.

STYLING

Look at the photograph: the 'trunks' are now developed and their side branches have been lightly trimmed and carefully wired. There is always a settling-in period following the initial planting before growth resumes at the normal rate. When this stage has been reached it is safe to style like this, not before. Trees that are not over-worked always do better and develop faster than those not allowed such recovery time. The rock planting must be shaded after the styling session and fed well to stimulate strong growth.

EVOLUTION

In the drawing I am visualizing the planting after about another five years' growth. Think of the rock as a sculpture representing the trunk of an old tree and the lines of the new growth as its branches. The shape of the new

Evolution: five years on.

trident maple

FIVE-TRUNK CLUMP STYLE

This planting was put together some years ago by Harvey Susuki of California as an experiment, in which he planted the maples on a very high (75–90cm/2½–3ft) piece of rotted tree fern bark, hoping to make it look like an old northwestern nurse log (a typical phenomenon of the Pacific Northwest, in which a fallen tree rots out and becomes a host for the regrowth of a diversity of plant forms). When Mr Susuki died, his wife gave the planting to Charlie and Ruth Anderson, who very carefully removed it from the tree fern bark. It took several years to get the maple roots down to a workable level so that it could be planted in a shallower pot.

Height of maples:
60cm (24in)
Age: 33 years
Size of container:
25 x 20 x 7.5cm (10 x 8 x 3in)
Colour of container:
mottled yellow glaze

Trident maple: five-trunk clump style.

The photograph of the original planting shows the trident maples in good health and shooting vigorously. The shape of the clump is pleasing and it gives a nice feeling of a natural grove. The flow and curvature of the trunks are also pleasing and they harmonize well together. The

After styling: the clump standing in a bigger pot.

different thicknesses of the trunks are an interesting aspect and, together with the varying heights, create a satisfying group arrangement. This kind of design is well within the reach of the novice and will give tremendous pleasure in its making and maintenance.

STYLING

After styling, the maples have more clearly defined trunk lines and the branches have been simplified by pruning knots of twigs and buds so that they look less congested.

Peripheral twig density is fine but even this needs thinning out to avoid the formation of swellings on the wood, as it buds prolifically. Wiring has lowered some of the extremely 'cupped' branch lines associated with upcurved young growth. Pruning and careful side wiring has opened and spread the branches so that the whole arrangement appears bigger and more graceful. You can see how much the planting has spread by the size of the original pot, which now looks tiny.

EVOLUTION

In the drawing the pot has been changed for a longer, wider and lower one. I have indicated a drippy glaze: off-white, smoky yellow or dull blue would all look wonderful with this arrangement. I have anticipated the fattening of the surfaced root mass, which can often be engineered simply by placing a moss pad over it – remember that wet roots will thicken (see page 93).

The canopy of the tree has been extended to reach a domed fullness that is entirely consistent with the existing design. The shorter trunks have been kept so but allowed some spread, and the shape of the curving negative area above them is particularly effective. The branch pattern has been encouraged to keep its kinks and quirks rather than be too smooth. Straight lines and changes of direction add character to the image.

Evolution: further growth and a change of pot.

chinese elm

SEVEN-TRUNK LANDSCAPE (SAIKEI)

This saikei (Japanese simulated natural landscape) was put together by the late Tim Patterson and is being maintained by Charlie and Ruth Anderson.

Height of elms: 12.5–25cm (5–10in)
Age: 5–15 years from imported material
Size of container: 60 x 37.5 x 7.5cm (24 x 15 x 3in)
Colour of container: blue/green glaze

This kind of grouping, where the trees are small but stocky, has a lot of power and interesting character. The placement of the trees has been well thought out and although they are short, the similarity of the trunks creates a strong visual link between them and an admirable unity. The group assembly is straightforward –

Chinese elm: seven-trunk landscape (saikei).

what sets this apart is the small stature of the trees and the effect this has on the perspective of the whole planting concept. Combined with the long form of the pot and the low tree line, the use of rocks and sand below the mossy hill make it appear as though one is out at sea or in the middle of a huge lake, looking towards the shore.

STYLING

After styling, the feeling of being away from shore is even stronger. Care has been taken to preserve Tim's concept, and pruning, thinning and wiring have reflected a natural refining of the design without any major changes. I looked long and hard before wire-shaping the branches, and aimed for a main massing of contours rather than a major re-shaping.

After styling.

EVOLUTION

In the drawing I was free to make some changes, but even here I have kept to the spirit of Tim's design because it reminds me quite forcibly of the image of ancient oak forests in Europe, where short trees with gnarled branches can be found on land that has been undisturbed for millennia.

I have made the major tree taller and with stronger lateral branch development. The styling of all the trees is mainly that of the broom (see page 63), but with a lot of internal branch line simplification. This thinning opens up the frame of branches and allows the eye to travel along branch lines, enjoying the changing directions. These abrupt changes are associated with the natural damage all trees face over the years and add a lot of quality to the image.

I have opened up the taller trees on the right more than the shorter ones on the left to give variety and to emphasize the low line receding into the distance. The major tree is the pivot of the whole thing – the just off-centre placement is pleasing to the eye and is subtler than the 'one-third' placement often talked about in general design. The pot is still too deep.

Evolution: the changes retain the spirit of the design.

'seiju' elm

NINE-TRUNK GROUP

This planting was put together by Charlie and Ruth Anderson about three to four years ago from material from Carl Young's nursery in Lodi, California. I was told it was the only group they ever tried to do together! 'Seiju' is a variety of Chinese elm raised by Carl and Shin Young.

Height of elms: 25–60cm (10–24in)
Age: 5–10 years
Size of container: 60 x 45 x 6.25cm (24 x 18 x 2½in)
Colour of container: grey/brown mica

'Seiju' elm: nine-tree group.

This design is one that utilizes the slender, tall trunks to good advantage. Very different to the previous group, it is another variation where the broom style shines (see page 63). The fine twigs and tiny leaves of this variety add even more to the illusion of immense size in this planting.

STYLING

After styling and thinning to restore the lightness to the design, you can see that the planting has regained its original structure. A heavy root on the major tree has been removed and there is a much nicer root line below it. The overall balance in the group is good and brings to mind an image of elms on the skyline or in a fold of distant hills – the British countryside used to be full of such images. The

After styling.

tiny leaves of 'Seiju' reinforce the scale concept of the distant clump.

Instead of a flat foreground, it can be really interesting to mound the soil so that it rises a little in front of the group, suggesting a scene dropping away downhill. This may be done 'straight-on' or by planting in a much longer pot and tapering the 'hill' slowly along the length of the container, or diagonally, so that the planting steps down into the distance. The possibilities are almost endless.

EVOLUTION

In the drawing I have rolled time forward another five years or so. All the changes here are extensions of what is already underway. Order has simply been restored to the random lines of the old growth, largely through wiring, and new growth lines have been allowed to develop strongly. Wiring and pruning produce the segmented, curving, fan-like forms seen here. Development consists of making cones of outflung branches and twigs. It is an interesting and fairly straightforward process, although it looks complex.

The chief differences lie in the heavier masses of branches and the careful use of negative areas to punctuate the mass and prevent it from closing in. 'Seiju' elms are willing and, like all compact varieties, need a light touch to thin them enough to keep them looking tree-like – if they get too dense they can begin to look like shrubs. Their habit of growth, with opposite shoot placement, looks oddly mechanical, but a little thinning out of visually obvious areas will do a lot to alleviate the problem. When new buds pop out, be sure to rub away promptly

any that are not needed to build density. This avoids the formation of those little swellings you can see up and down the trunks in the photograph.

If you read the explanation of how the broom is developed (see page 63), you will find that the phrase 'reversed umbrella' shape describes exactly what you have to do. Encourage upright, narrowly splayed-out branch lines, which you control by wiring and periodic pinching. Remove in-facing buds and keep out-facing growths small and pleasingly spaced along the ascending branch lines. This gives the series of gently out-flowing lines that diffuse upwards from the main structures. Periodic thinning and trimming maintains daintiness of growth habit and dissuades any 'heroes' among the branches.

If you look carefully at the drawing, you can see where some internal branch structures are heavy with twigs while others are cleaned out. This gives variety and enables you to design with the relative densities throughout the planting. Think of it like fan-vaulting supporting a church ceiling, with some of the areas between the ribs open while others are filled in.

Evolution: five years on.

The other big difference is in the container – I have chosen a much longer, broader and shallower rectangle. A light colour would work: the Japanese unglazed light grey would be good, while a pot in off-white crackle glaze (as used by English potter Gordon Duffett), would be quite wonderful. The extra front-to-back space provides a better open area at the front and a perceivable sense of depth to the group.

western hemlock

FIVE-TRUNK GROUP ON ROCK

Charlie and Ruth Anderson acquired this group from the late Tim Patterson. When he became ill, the trees were very much neglected and several of them died. Charlie repotted, replanted and redesigned the group, and now it is coming back to vigorous life.

Height of hemlocks: 15–35cm (6–14in)
Age: 5–6 years
Size of rock: 75 x 22.5 x 15cm (30 x 9 x 6in)

The rock is the overwhelming element in this planting. When we came to our photographic session, the comment was made that the rock might well have been used the other way up! When a rock is this interesting, one way to handle it is to downplay the plant material and keep it simple in form, so that the rock and trees do not fight for equal attention. How do we do that? One way is to style the

Western hemlock: five-trunk group on rock.

trees to emphasize their lateral movement, so that the feeling is more of horizontal planes that tie the trees to the movement of the rock. In the first photograph, the immature upright trunks look perched on top of the rock and appear unlinked to it. Potentially, of course, the group could be wonderful.

STYLING

I first checked the health of the trees carefully and then decided to wire them fairly extensively. I concentrated on making the lines of trunks and branches flow together, and tried to lower the lines as I worked to get the foliage down closer to the rock face. Unnecessary foliage – any hanging or rising leaves that were breaking the visual line of the branches when they were wired into place – was pruned away. (Always trim *after* lowering branches into their new positions, as you may want some of that extension growth to fill out a line. Overall, I may have removed about 10 per cent of the foliage bulk.)

The trick in this sort of restyling with such small material is never to strip the trees down to nothing. Over-thinning, although widely practised in the initial stages in bonsai, is horticultural illiteracy. The tree needs those leaves and many fail to survive. I know Charlie and Ruth to be excellent bonsai people who really understand and utilize dappled shade for their trees, and so I was quite happy to thin out the trees as shown. The plant-stress aspect of my work lay in the wiring, because this opens the bark at the points of bending, and the moisture-conserving shade is kind to plants recovering from wiring.

EVOLUTION

In the drawing I have imagined the planting in about seven years' time. When the planting was restyled, I designed the branches so that this type of shortened and spreading contour line could easily be developed. I have added another two trunks to build up foliage density and add interest to the long negative area below the whole canopy of branches.

The low, undulating foliage line ties in with the shape of the rock, and once again the device of diminishing tree size has been used to conjure up a feeling of distance. The form of the larger trees on the left is repeated twice: in the middle of the planting its size is

After styling.

reduced by half, and then by half again at the right side. Advantage has been taken of the opportunity to play with the relative heights of the three areas and to introduce smaller negative areas to break up the mass.

The image works as a symbol of a rocky island and would look superb if displayed standing in a long, shallow suiban (undrained decorative pot) filled with water, when the reflection of the arched stone would look marvellous. It could also be displayed on a sheet of smoked glass for a richer, moodier result – and just think of the effect if it were lit with the beam of a low-heat spotlight that would pick up the texture of both leaves and rock.

Evolution: seven years on.

'kingsville' box

11-TREE LANDSCAPE

Genieve and Jack Enwright purchased the original tree for this landscape 25 years ago from Connie Derderian in Boston, who was curator of the Anderson collection at the Arnold Arboretum. At the time, this variety of box (Buxus sempervirens 'Kingsville') was fairly new in bonsai. The smaller trees are cuttings from the original one. The rocks are from Vermont and were chosen for their rugged texture.

Height of box: 7.5–25cm (3–10in)
Age: 10–25 years
Size of container: 45 x 35 x 5cm (18 x 14 x 2in)
Colour of container: brown unglazed

This scene suggests a mountain river edged with boulders. As you look at it, even the texture of the gravel used in the river bed recalls the movement of water in the way it creates a visual flicker. Sharp mounding of the soil used in conjunction with the different heights of the planting successfully adds to the movement of the landscape.

The planting area itself is crescent-shaped, wrapping around the river bed to emphasize its flatness. The dispersal of trunks around the banks of the river bed is varied and interesting, and the different sizes of the trunks and their spread of foliage all serve to focus attention on the central idea. The negative space in this landscape is very

'Kingsville' box: 11-tree landscape.

well used and adds considerably to the beauty of the design. All this takes place inside a tiny spread of soil. It feels infinite, yet remains essentially an intimate close-up of a river bend.

The rear view shows how in a good design even the back elevations of the trees are thought about, trained to be varied and could form a very acceptable basis for a new group planting. These elements add a tremendously satisfying depth to the overall concept.

STYLING

'Kingsville' box are very pretty and their growth habit is compact and pleasing, but they do tend to 'fill in' trained lines with new growth. When they are groomed by thinning over-dense areas, their lovely delicate structure and mantle of tiny leaves can be properly appreciated.

EVOLUTION

The drawing shows how such a planting can be changed and subtly altered by the use of a longer pot and a few

Rear view.

extra plants. I am imagining it in about five years' time – the trees have been developed further and extra trees extend existing foliage lines and suggest greater space. The forms of the foliage remain shallow 'mushrooms' that blend with the contours of the soil. Subtle use has been made of the negative areas to add punctuation to the spreading green mass.

Evolution: five years on.

japanese maple

11-TRUNK LANDSCAPE/GROUP

This group was grown by Genieve and Jack Enwright from cuttings taken 20 years ago from another maple grove. Genieve told me that the rooted cuttings were put on the back of the rock with a small amount of soil, and located and tied in with wire screening.

Height of maples: 20–30 cm (8–12in)
Age: 20 years
Size of rock: 37.5 x 10 x 15cm (15 x 4 x 6in)
Size of container: 50 x 37.5 x 5cm (20 x 15 x 2in)
Colour of container: brown unglazed

The photograph below shows the grove before trimming. The new growth is splendidly healthy and has that deep red flush associated with well-maintained maples. The set-up is already very interesting and creates a familiar scene of a clump of trees in a hilly meadow, with the line of trees following the high rocky outcrop. The trunk lines are very well related to each other in form and there is a good variety of thicks and thins in close proximity.

Japanese maple: 11-trunk landscape/group.

STYLING

After styling, the maples are less bulky and the negative space is restored here and there through the dense canopy of leaves. Thinning out the leaves like this draws attention to the spaces throughout the planting. Look at the great trunk bases with their strong root flare: they seem suddenly to have jumped into prominence now that the window effect of the more open lines has been created.

EVOLUTION

The next stage in shaping this maple landscape is to heighten that pleasing sense of the quiet pastoral scene. I have drawn the grouping with a wider line. The down-sweeping outer canopy echoes, in a way, the shape of the hill. This means that an interesting band of negative space is generated between the soil and the underline of the foliage. It might be fun to interrupt that space with extra trunk lines at some stage. This, of course, would give the opportunity to extend the foliage lines too – perhaps even to introduce another group of diminutive maples, implying still greater space.

Depth is an interesting concept to play with in such a restricted space. Suppose, for instance, that the length of the pot were to be doubled: think of the space and how it might be used! One very British idea that comes to mind is to introduce a hedge line right in front of the trees in the foreground, to accentuate the feeling of seeing the group on the far side of a field or fields and suggest the open quality of rolling farmland.

After styling.

Evolution: developing width and depth.

european hornbeam

MULTI-TRUNK GROUP

Genieve and Jack Enwright were given this delightful hornbeam group by their teacher Connie Derderian from Boston, who was one of the early practitioners of bonsai in the US. There was very little knowledge of bonsai in the States when Connie first wanted to learn about it. On hearing that someone at the Brooklyn Botanic Garden in New York was giving instruction, she moved there, took lessons, and developed this hornbeam group from about 40 rooted cuttings that she bought. It was one of the first things made by Connie, about 50 years ago.

Height of hornbeams: 15–67.5cm (6–27in)
Age: 50 years approx.
Size of container: 55 x 40 x 5cm (22 x 16 x 2in)
Colour of container: brown, unglazed

Opposite: *European hornbeam: multi-trunk group, after styling.*

STYLING

As I groomed these trees for the photograph, I respected the owners' request that the group stay largely in the original form. I just worked on opening up some negative space in the dense green and superficially pruning some indentations that were big enough to generate shadows across the leaf planes. It was wonderful to have the opportunity to work on an authentic western bonsai with a known history.

EVOLUTION

I think the group could be developed into a fabulous form and still keep the spirit of Connie's work simply by allowing the branches to round out the leaf contours a little more at both edges. It is also crying out for a larger pot! It would be nice to team the wider image with a wider pot from one of the great English potters.

Evolution: rounding out the contours.

american larch

11-TRUNK GROUP

Genieve and Jack Enwright collected these larches as small roadside trees on a visit to Maine. They brought them home, planted them and skilfully developed them into this strong image of stately forest trees.

Height of larches: 20–65cm (8–26in)
Age: 10–15 years
Size of container: 45 x 35 x 5cm (18 x 14 x 2in)
Colour of container: muted yellow glaze

Opposite: *American larch: 11-trunk group, after styling.*

Evolution: developing as planned.

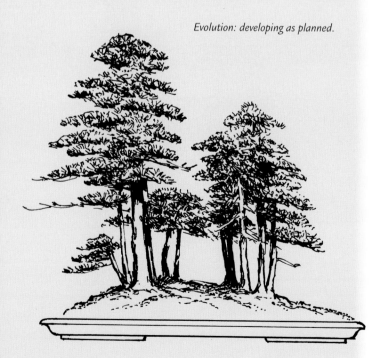

STYLING

The photograph was taken after a styling session in which I thinned excess buds and branches at branch/trunk junctions, cleaned branch underlines and did a little bit of wiring to accentuate the differences in branch length. As you can see, there is a very pleasing twin group of trunks with the dominant, taller and heavier of the two on the left, beginning a narrow spired outline that is repeated through the arrangement. The trick is to maintain that feeling but to allow individual horizontal branch lines to pierce the conical contour periodically to keep the design diverse.

It is very easy to let such a group become a bit mechanical. With a species like this that is so willing to bud for you, it is essential to guard against mindless pruning back. I developed the small tree at the bottom left by pruning away a blocking line and then wiring another into a tiny tree form.

The surface roots of this arrangement are excellent. Just like those of the Japanese maple 11-trunk group (see page 20), they spread and connect the trunks in a very natural way, really tying the trunks into the ground like old trees in the forest.

EVOLUTION

In the drawing, I have visualized the planting developed exactly along the lines that Jack and Genieve have planned. I have added more height on the left, and the horizontals have been extended a little but not too much. It is interesting to keep the illusion of extreme height and this works best if the branches remain compact in relation to the shafts of the trunk. It encourages the viewer to think of huge trunks with narrow peripheries of foliage.

I have increased the pot size a little to add breadth under the eaves of the forest. In such an image, a few peeled and silvered branches can subtly reflect the effects of storm damage, and sometimes even an entire trunk may die and remain as a ghost tree. Used with restraint, this type of visual keynote is interesting, but keep it to a minimum; otherwise it will lose its impact. If you carve, do it so that the area blends in, and 'grey' it down with watercolour paint (see page 60). Never leave it treated bone-white with lime sulphur, as this will jump forward too much.

'yatsubusa' japanese maple

MULTI-TRUNK ROOT-CONNECTED GROUP

I imported this maple (yatsubusa means dwarf or compact) in 1984 from Fukukaen Nursery in Nagoya, Japan. At the time it was described as follows:

Height of maple: 52.5 (21in)
Width of maple: 101cm (40in)
Age: 35 years (ten was probably closer)

The pot was a complete disaster and looked more like a child's pinch pot than a serious container supplied for a tree with this potential. It was a simulated stone container and the tree immediately looked like what the Scots refer to as 'nippit' in the pot – constrained and tight-looking, rather than 'happily' planted. The tree certainly did well horticulturally, though, and quickly expanded its excellent flat and dense root system to fill the 'pinch pot' to its capacity. At that time I had no other container big enough to house the root system and I was stuck with it – temporarily. The sandstone rock image implied by the ochre/purple finish was far too heavy a combination with the dainty, compact nature of the green foliage mass. It seemed obvious that a simple light grey oval would be a better way to go.

The root-connected base was very interesting but the line it made was, to say the least, monotonously straight. I considered several corrective options for this unrelenting straightness, the one that jumped out at me being to plant it diagonally. The trouble with that was the length of the root line – to achieve a diagonal line that looked sensible, I would have needed a huge pot. Then the solution came – cut it into two sections!

RESTYLING THE TRUNK

I repotted the maple in early 1985, just as the buds were opening. With dwarf maples, this usually means late winter. The light grey unglazed pot measured 70 x 45 x 5cm (28 x 18 x 2in). I root-pruned the tree, cutting the roots well back and taking care to sever all the major root tips. The root mass on these dwarf maples is often as dense as plywood! I then pruned out some of the dense thicket of trunks along the major root line and sealed all the pruning cuts.

Opposite: *Yatsubusa Japanese maple: multi-trunk root-connected group, summer 1985. The dimensions are still largely as given in 1984.*

The next step was to consider carefully where to divide the base line of the trunk. Eventually I located the point at roughly the two-thirds mark and sawed the trunk in two, dividing the root pad as well. I then planted it as a 'disconnected V', with the point facing to the back. As it was laid in the pot for the first time as a twin unit, it was immediately transformed from just another 'import' into a tree of some individual character. Quite by accident, I had found just the right treatment to minimize the awkward-looking

growth pattern often seen in dwarf tree types. It now looked like an avenue of the sort you find when walking through a wood. This intuitive kind of breakthrough is one of the nicest rewards in bonsai, although it does not happen often – or at least, not to me!

I sealed the two exposed trunk cuts and removed extra branches that had suddenly become in-facing and were blocking the new vista between the trunks. It became apparent that a lot of branches, suddenly made out-facing,

had a great deal of growing to do and a lot of extension was needed. (Note: always prune the roots first. Then prune the trunk and branches, *before* watering in – this prevents the tree from weeping and losing strength.)

The transplanting was completed and the tree took off like a rocket – both halves competing for the lion's share of the fresh soil.

THINNING

With all these changes in mind, the foliage was thinned in the summer to open and lighten the tiering between branch levels. It was wired so that extending lines could be placed precisely. I could then plan each tree profile as a planed and natural maple form. The branches do become heavy with leaves and grooming them can be confusing: what worked for me was to part the leaves and identify the branch lines with my fingers, then to remove dangling leaves and shoots and any that masked the rounded upper profiles, always pulling gently *with the direction of growth*. Do this around early summer, waiting until the leaves are just set and fully hardened.

If you look at the photograph you can see elements of shadowing dividing the overall leaf mass into branch planes. This is the result of the technique just described. You can by all means thin out more, but my aim at this point was still to extend the branch planes, and 'skinny-ing' everything out retards development. The trick in keeping all the dwarf maples happy once they are potted is to maintain the balance of moisture, and overthinning is dangerous. After each operation on the tree, it was returned to the polytunnel (hoop-house) and shaded until it budded out again.

Later each summer the tree should be groomed again but this time using pruning shears, as the growth will be hard and will break if the fingers are used. The routine is to part the leaves and check for any 'heroes' among the new shoots. These are eradicated quickly unless you want to extend lines at that point. The next aim is to reduce the sheer numbers of new twigs emerging close in to the trunk lines. It is like thinning a broom style tree (see page 63): dwarf maples need the same windows of negative space around their trunk/branch junctions. While thinning the branches, opposite twigs and sub-branches are also removed, as this does a lot to reduce the mechanically perfect look of the dwarf plant.

In 1986 the maple was repotted again to narrow the 'V' formation and make better use of the space in the pot.

Root disturbance was kept very light, but even in a year the two halves of the root pad had welded themselves together.

DEVELOPMENT

Thirteen years later, in 1998, the maple had achieved a satisfying design. The bases had become heavy and the grove of 'trees' had matured into a settled form. The balance of finer branch growth had also come a long way.

EVOLUTION

One way to add another dimension to the design might be to encourage the tallest trunk to grow taller. If the mass on the left was also allowed to rise but still stayed below the tallest and the right-hand mass was kept constant in height, a great increase in perspective would result. The movement through the planting could be further enhanced if the extreme right periphery were lowered a little and extended to the right.

The pattern of the root lines has no small part to play in all this and the formation continues to add immeasurably to this fascinating image of an ageing deciduous forest. I have drawn it out of leaf to highlight the sheer pattern of the grove and the satisfaction of seeing such a forest close at hand.

Evolution: encouraging height.

'catlin' elm

33-TRUNK GROVE

'Catlin' elm (Ulmus parvifolia 'Catlin') is widely grown in the US as bonsai. It was named after John Catlin of La Canada, California, who discovered and propagated this small-leaved, dark green form of Chinese elm. This famous group of trees from the Pacific Rim Bonsai Collection was created by Melba Tucker of El Monte, California in 1973.

Height of elms: 20–60cm (8–24in)
Age: 25 years
Size of slab: 75 x 45 x 3.75cm (30 x 18 x 1½in)

Catlin elm: 33-trunk grove.

This is a fine example of the group or grove arrangement and has been carefully developed over the years so that everything works together in an ideal way. The lattice of trunks with their thicks and thins, and the way the horizontal bars of dark green leaves cross them, are very convincing as a statement about quiet groves everywhere. It is quite enchanting.

On the practical side, these elms can be tricky to handle as their growth habit can seem a little stiff. But this has been adroitly side-stepped here, where the foliage pads have been trained to sit on the branches in an entirely natural way. If the ascendant growth habit shows anywhere, it is in the depth of some of the pads, where if a flatter line is encouraged it may work better for the group in the long term.

The important aspect of Melba's work is the artistic concept, which is hard to beat. What Melba has already said so well with this grove needs no further development of mine!

'san josé' juniper

THREE-TRUNK JAPANESE SAIKEI

This saikei was created by Mr Kaz Yoneda and donated to the Pacific Rim Bonsai Collection in honour of its opening. It was designed in 1982 using three nursery plants and lace rock gathered in California.

Height of junipers: 25, 45, 55cm (10, 18, 22in)
Age: 20–26 years approx.
Size of container: 70 x 50 x 4.5cm (28 x 20 x 1¾in)
Colour of container: brown unglazed

The miniature landscape seen here is another interpretation of a river-bank scene. The gravel symbolizes a river-bed and the dwarf mondo grass (*Ophiopogon japonicus* var. 'Nana' or *O. j.* 'Kyoto Dwarf') lends a marsh reed-like texture to the transition zone between the river and the mounded banks.

The trunk lines of the trees are full of movement and the taller lace rock stabilizes the design very well. It stands

'San José' juniper: three-trunk Japanese saikei.

there like a massive tree, and the main juniper beside it has been styled so that it seems to flow from it in a very natural way. The second and third trunks successfully step down in size and scale, suggesting distance. The negative spaces are getting a little blurred and perhaps need some opening up.

Like the 'Kingsville' box (see page 18), this is a species that soon 'fills in', but it is difficult, perhaps even undesirable, to attempt to maintain an original design without allowing some natural changes to occur.

EVOLUTION

In the spirit of creativity, I thought it might be fun to take the bones of the original design and use them as the core of a larger design. The top drawing shows what could happen if you planted the landscape on a customized ciment fondu slab and added more trees. I am guessing the slab size to be around 105 x 50 x 7.5cm (42 x 20 x 3in).

Making the slab from ciment fondu and fibre-glass cloth over an aluminium wire armature (see Chapter 6), will mean that the structure is fairly lightweight but strong. I have found it useful to incorporate some projecting wire loops into the top layer of cement to help in tying the trees safely and accurately on to the slab.

Consider sinking some metal tubes into the 'floor' portion of the planting zone as you make the slab, to act as drainage pipes. If you sink the 'floor' of the planting zone itself, the recessed part will act as a low wall. This retains the soil and plants and prevents them from spreading. Place drainage mesh (see page 67) over the drain pipes.

In the second drawing I have added ten extra junipers, five on each side. When you put together a concept like this you will find it a great deal easier if you construct a custom-fitted mesh planting grid (see page 67). If you make it out of heavy aluminium wire you can bend it to suit the rise and fall of the floor of the slab. It certainly helps to pre-wire and prune the trees so that once the trees are in position you need only adjust angles and fine-tune the foliage pads with scissors to neaten the profiles.

When placing the plants at this stage you would need to provide the right degree of trunk proximity – check those negative areas! You should neither overcrowd, nor plant so wide apart that you lose the value of the trunk lines coming together. The arrangement is shown in the drawing at the bottom and the plan. Instructions for planting, and adding rocks and accessory plants, are given on page 112.

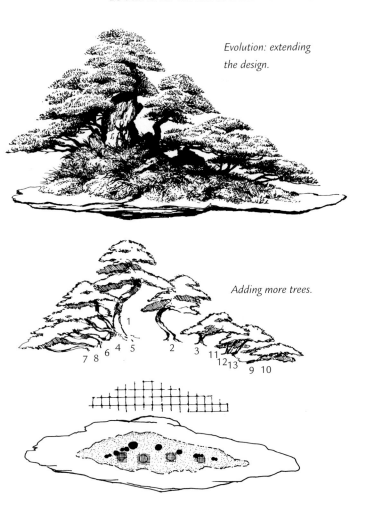

Evolution: extending the design.

Adding more trees.

Planting and drainage positions, plus location grid.

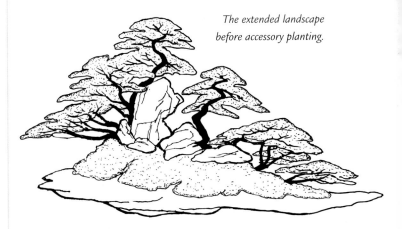

The extended landscape before accessory planting.

The original river bed has now gone, but in its place the strata on the edge of the 'rock' add a lot of lateral movement. Extra mondo grass, tiny-featured azaleas like *Rhododendron serpyllifolium*, ferns and mosses add texture and character. Take care not to overplant the slab – remember to leave some empty space on each side.

trident maple

11-TRUNK RAFT GROUP

The dimensions below give the current size of this impressive raft group but, as you will see, it has had a chequered history!

Height of maple: 60cm (24in)
Width of maple: 100cm (40in)
Base trunk diameter: 7.5cm (3in)
Age: 100 years +

I first saw this tree in 1967 at the nursery of Bromage and Young in Guildford, Surrey. The tree stood in a potting shed and was covered in white flags. Apart from the fabulous core of the trunk, it looked almost flat! Closer inspection showed the flags to be marking where whole trunks and major branches had been broken right off the plant. The debris of bits laid on the bench was quite depressing; the flags were for the inevitable insurance claim. It turned out that the tree had travelled from Japan to Guildford unsecured in the crate and that its own shifting weight had crushed all the superstructure of this once magnificent raft. The then owner was similarly crushed by this conversion of star to stump! I vowed then that I would one day have this tree.

Four years later I acquired it, after he had given up. Remember that there was very little bonsai knowledge around at the time. We were all operating in the dark – the technical input, both good and bad, was to come much later. I was young and inexperienced enough to take on the tree armed only with a real love of maples and a sense of having time to redevelop it. The first owner had done very well to restart the branching, but of course it all looked very tentative at that stage.

REDEVELOPMENT

When I first worked on the tree it fitted the original pot from Japan, which measured 53 x 25 x 5cm (21 x 10 x 2in)! My first steps were to feed the tree heavily and to maintain constant soil dampness. With such a limited root-run, the tree was pretty root-bound.

In spring 1972 I changed the pot for one with greater width and depth. At the same time, after an initial impatient winter of checking and re-checking the design, I decided to reverse the tree and feature the present front for the first time. I washed and combed the roots first and cut away the 'horse's collar' of pot-girdling outer roots that is produced by all vigorous trident maples. The soil was mounded to tilt the tree, raising the present front at the left-hand edge. This gave greater visual separation between the trunks and also increased the perspective. I carefully sorted out the roots, spreading more than pruning them. The maple settled happily and grew so much that I had constantly to direct its energy by means of selective pruning and wiring.

By checking very carefully on the sort of styling that the few undamaged parts of the tree had received, it was possible to deduce (nothing in writing at this time, remember) that the tree had been styled by permitting new growth to make enough extension to be wired. Then it was trimmed back several times and finally reduced quite hard at the end of each season.

I tried, by trial and error, to resurrect such a system. The tree was allowed an initial shoot extension of three pairs of leaves each year. This overall extension was wired and then allowed to grow away unchecked until the wires became tight. The wires were then removed and each wire-curved form cut short, maybe back to two pairs of leaves, trying always to cut back to a point above a latent bud that would produce growth in such a way as to give an attractive change of direction. The new shoots from the latent buds were encouraged to make two or three pairs of leaves and were then cut short without wiring. The wired and non-wired lines gave a pleasant mix of curved and straight lines. At the end of the season, the current year's growth was pruned hard back, retaining a scant 5cm (2in) of 'spurs'. (The little shortened branch lines actually had a charm of

their own and I experimented on their development with very tiny trident maples, but that is another story.)

I attempted simply to make the new branch system a logical extension of how the original branches may have appeared, based on the shape and position of the stumps. Growth consolidated with each season and tentative branch lines began to assume character and take on taper. I switched techniques to give the tree a rest and for a couple of years concentrated on soft-pinching new growth, which soon bulked out the contours.

I tried to flatten the lines of each branch by extending its main line and keeping the crown of each profile shallow. Each autumn the branches were spur-pruned to keep them short and the cuts were sealed. A bonus of this was the ongoing vigour of the inner branches: each pruning redirected the energy back through the branches.

The pot was changed a number of times to suit the steadily extending tree: maples like to have an underpinning area of root-run below extending branch lines. The original banked-up soil area was soon permeated with roots that held the tree comfortably at the new angle. The

Trident maple: 11-trunk raft group, winter 1997/8.

original surface roots in this area have now fattened up tremendously to become landmark features of the tree. The base trunk diameter has thickened significantly and the bark is witnessing the expansion with cracking and exfoliation. The other surface roots have vastly thickened and add further beauty to the old tree.

THE CONTAINER

The wonderful pot by Gordon Duffett in which the raft is now displayed has the aesthetic value of the old pots from China, Korea and Japan. Gordon fires his pots to 1280°C. For glaze colours and textures, he refers to twelfth- and thirteenth-century ceramics and early Japanese Bizen and Iga ware. He also likes his pots to reveal something of the stresses caused by the high temperature. Because hand-building techniques are used, each pot is unique, and this – along with a cross combination of various clay bodies and glazes – ensures that no two pots look alike.

A good pot is the final touch in creating an image, and as the tree ages it is essential to provide a really fine frame such as this magnificent pot. The muted ochres and greys are a beautiful combination with the colours in the old bark.

EVOLUTION

In the drawing above, I see the trunks being featured more. Lightening of the foliage pads close in to the trunks will shift the visual weight, giving the foliage pads the appearance of spreading further along existing lines. The interior thinning, combined with a little more extension of the periphery, will give a very maple-like lightness to the image.

The raft in summer 1998, newly trimmed for exhibition.

tools and materials

Re-creating a tiny version of a favourite scene may seem impossibly difficult, yet all it really takes is to assemble a few easily obtained plants, perhaps some rocks and mosses, and a suitable container – and even that you can make yourself (see Chapter 6)! After that, maintaining the plants in their new 'landscape' calls for exactly the same techniques as those used for individual bonsai, and these are described in full in the following pages.

So let's start by taking a look at the various components of a miniature landscape.

PLANTS

The plants you choose for your landscape do not have to be wonderful and expensive examples or exotic species.

Most small landscapes employ trees, or plants with a tree-like image. The plants used mostly fall within the 5–30cm (2–12in) height range. Generally, small-leaved conifers work well as their tiny features are in scale, but deciduous trees can also be used for their mood and colour. In Chapter 3 you will find suggestions for suitable species, guidance on identifying good examples and where to find them, and warnings of some of the snags you may encounter. The Tree Care Directory provides notes on how to look after the plants throughout the year.

Accessory Plants

Various small plants, grasses and mosses can be used to create surface texture and mood. Collecting these can become a hobby in itself.

Accent Plants

Accent plants differ from accessory plants in that they extend the mood of the landscape by their colour and shape. They are displayed separately beside the landscape, and the colour of their flowers and the pots in which they are placed add a natural feeling to the plantings. As you study the photographs of these small plants scattered throughout the book, another hobby may beckon – and just look at those tiny pots, too!

ROCKS

Small rocks and stones can be used in a landscape to suggest and to build cliffs, ravines and coast-lines, or simply to embellish the soil surface. The vital points to look for are muted colour and a form that blends in without dominating the composition – unless, of course, it is to be the main feature. Grey, black and shades of brown all work well if they are not too bright: strident colour 'jumps' forward and destroys the sense of perspective that quiet colours suggest. The stone should have interesting folds and crevices, rather than being smooth like a cobble stone.

SOIL

Planting soil should be of the open, spongy type preferred for all bonsai, with a structure that encourages good drainage.

Soil Components

Peat

Composted peat may be combined with a little topsoil and mixed to a paste with water for adding special contours, such as steep hillsides, to land-scapes, as it will provide a 'key' when applying the final coat of mosses. Peat may also be used as part of the general potting mix.

Akadama (Japanese red soil)

This is a subsoil from Japan that is used in great quantities by bonsai growers everywhere. When fresh, it holds its pea-like structure very well, but you should be on your guard against acquiring recycled soil that may have lost this desirable characteristic. Akadama will provide a water reservoir for plants in hot locations and climates, but take care to follow the proportions suggested for individual species in the Tree Care Directory.

Leaf mould

Oak or beech leaf mould is a mellow organic material that trees enjoy very much.

Sand

Fine rounded sand combined with sharper sand forms the 'mixed sand' used in the potting mixes in this book. Aim for rounded and sharp particles of between pinhead and match-head size (see page 55). In the UK, fine aquarium gravel works admirably for the rounded sand ingredient; in the US, chicken grit would be ideal. Sieved fine sand can be used as a topdressing to enhance the sense of scale and, where appropriate, to suggest water.

CONTAINERS

The mood of the landscape is heightened by the shape and proportions of its container. Ovals and rectangles are widely used, although others such as rounds and even petal-form pots can work well with some rocky scenes. A long container, allowing space for the planting and some over, is a favourite shape.

The pots used for planting bonsai groups work well for most landscapes. Such large bonsai pots tend to be expensive, but they do set off the landscape like a picture frame. Suitable containers, and particularly rock planters, may also be made at home with ciment fondu and fibre-glass cloth, and are great fun to do (see Chapter 6). Of course, not all landscapes need be huge, nor does the pot have to be big – it is really a question of proportion, and of creating the illusion of mood and place.

TOOLS AND SUNDRIES

To create a miniature landscape, you will need some of the tools made for general use in bonsai, as they make the jobs of pruning and plant maintenance much easier.

A pair of trimming shears, a wire cutter, branch pruners and a couple of rolls of aluminium training wire in 1mm, 1.5mm and 2mm gauges are indispensable. A rake is useful for combing out roots. A soil sieve with 6mm, 3mm and 1.5mm (¼in, ⅛in and ⅟₁₆in) meshes is handy for screening out coarse and fine soil material.

You will also need a good wound sealant. From Japan come a battleship-grey putty called Cut Wound Paste and a more liquid preparation called Kiyonal, and both are good. A German product called Lac-Balsam combines the easy application of Kiyonal with the grey bark-matching colour of Cut Wound Paste, and in my opinion this is the best of the three.

All the above items are available through the bonsai trade.

Accent plant: sisyrinchium. Red/brown free-form pot by Dan Barton. The shape resembles a rocky bank dotted with clumps of purple flowers.

FEED

To keep your plants in good condition, you will need liquid fertilizers such as Miracid, Miracle-Gro, Fish Emulsion and 0–10–10. The first three are given at the standard dilution unless otherwise specified; 0–10–10 is given at a dilution of 1 tablespoon to 3.5 litres (8 pints) of water, which is a ratio of 1:600. Trace Element Frit is a powdered compound containing all the micronutrients needed for sound plant growth. Give half a teaspoon annually to a pot, usually in spring.

choosing the plants

So where can you find the plants you need to start creating your miniature landscape? Most good garden centres should have suitable material in the sizes you need, but if you want more specialized types, bonsai nurseries are a good source. Other ways to acquire the plants you need are to collect them from the wild or to propagate them yourself.

SELECTING PLANTS

The main features to look for when selecting plants are:

- Small overall size (5–30cm/2–12in), although this will depend on your project.
- Compact growth.
- Small leaves.
- Characterful trunk.
- Surface roots.
- A shape that matches your design concept.

Accent plant: dwarf iris and self-seeded wild geranium. Pot by Phyl Barton. The profusion of wild flowers makes a wonderful combination with the simple pot.

- For groups, a common theme in the shapes chosen and some variety in trunk thickness.

Garden Centres

Most garden centres do a good job, but you should be aware of some problems that may arise. When selecting plants from a garden centre, there are three important areas to look at.

Foliage condition

First, check the state of the foliage carefully. The colour should be deep and even with no conspicuous yellowing or browned areas. The leaves should feel soft to the touch, or at least pliable: there is a difference between the feel of dried-up, desiccated leaves and those which are still active, even when the tree has sharply pointed needles. On an evergreen, check for brown, falling inner leaves, and if there are a great number in relation to the active green parts, pass it by, as this can indicate poor watering and/or a root-bound condition, where the tree has dried out as a result of insufficient water. It can also indicate damage from red spider or scale insects (see below).

Insect damage

Red spider If there is a yellow/greying discoloration of the foliage, check for red spider. Place something light coloured under a branch and tap the leaves: the insects will fall and you will see a dusting of moving red, like mobile cayenne pepper. If the plant is not too badly affected, it can be treated with insecticide, but it will take a year or two to regain full colour.

Scale insects These are sap-feeders that cause yellowing of the foliage and a generally 'tired' look to the plant. Check for pod-like shells on the backs of leaves and branches. These outer cases are hard, and the females carry white eggs below their bodies that make them look as though they are sitting on wads of lint.

Scale insects come in many shapes, sizes and colours. Their appearance usually blends well with their food source, so look carefully. I remember feeling smug about the bud set on a yew, only to have it die the same year. The orange 'buds' were actually scale insects, wonderfully disguised!

Aphids These pests are everywhere. The type that attack pines are woolly aphids, which to a casual glance resemble cigarette ash, and there are lots of others. Their attacks are not serious if treated promptly. The problem is that the 'honeydew' or sap secretion that all aphids produce not only attracts ants but can cause sooty mould to form, and this is bad news. Treat with an insecticide.

Scale insect eggs.

Aphids.

Using insecticides Volck is an environmentally friendly oil/water compound that operates by suffocating the insects. This is a great advantage, as pests cannot get used to it and build immunity because it smothers rather than poisons them. You need to withhold water the day before, on the day of spraying, and the day after spraying. This avoids damaging the plant, as the spray temporarily seals its breathing surfaces and an over-moist plant cannot lose the excess. Volck is otherwise safe and easy to use and is effective on a wide range of plants.

Other insecticides will also work for common pests, but do not get malathion spray anywhere near any deciduous tree – although it is often recommended, it turns most deciduous species into 'potato crisp' trees, as the leaf scorch is horrendous. Do not inhale malathion – it is very bad for you! Spray in calm air and use a coarse spray that will not drift. Wear a mask and wash your skin afterwards.

Root condition

In garden centres, two main problems may arise. The first is that of uneven or inadequate moisture, caused when plants are crowded together, which can lead to leaf scorch when blocks of plants are unevenly watered in full sun.

The second problem appears where stock is held over from year to year and becomes more and more root-bound. Often the trees arrive from a nursery, where they have been lifted from the open ground and root-wrapped prior to shipping to the garden centre. The garden centre staff then 'pot' them by popping the plants just as they are into a pot with enough soil around the root-wrapping to keep the roots moist. If there is a quick sale, all is well: the roots are unwrapped and spread, and the tree is planted and flourishes. However, if the plant hangs around unsold, roots pass through the wrapping into the outer temporary soil and form an encircling collar in the pot. This is not life threatening but quite difficult to deal with, so avoid such plants if there are alternatives. Problem plants can often be identified by a ring of sacking (burlap) peeking out of the soil, and they feel very firm in the pot.

Another thing that happens when a plant stands on unpaved ground for a season is that roots grow through the drainage holes in the pot and rapidly become large tap roots. The inner roots are bypassed and, if the condition goes unchecked, deteriorate as they become redundant. So, wiggle the container and if it is really 'rooted through', find one that is not.

You can correct all the problems described above if they are not too severe, but you should be aware that it will take time.

Bonsai Nurseries

All the observations made above about garden centres apply here too, and these nurseries too generally do an excellent job.

Bonsai nurseries present great opportunities for the miniature landscaper – and for the owner, who may be rather too attentive, so wait for the excitement of your arrival to die down and then walk round quietly on your own! Many nurseries feature imported trees from Japan and China, and the better ones are very good indeed, but others may be less than satisfactory. So how can you make a judgement? Let's set up some criteria.

Trunk

You are looking for the smaller trees and you are going to find a lot of trunks that are better designated as 'stems' due to their immature appearance.

Look for some trunk taper – difficult to find in such small plants, but not impossible. Often, to achieve taper the plant will have been chopped off and a lateral branch regrown in its place, creating a step down in thickness. This process may have been repeated three or four times on some trees, which is fine. The idea is to generate character in the young tree and to create the gnarled appearance of age. Avoid trees that have no taper.

Usually, trunk chopping is accompanied by wire-shaping. You will often find the imported tree still coiled with wire. This is also fine – provided that the wire has not bedded in and scarred the trunk. Avoid such trees.

Sometimes small plants will have dead wood featured on them as a carved and/or silvered area. These 'natural' wounds can either add a lot of character to the tree or be the ruination of it, according to how well the process has been carried out. If the tree has been carved recently – you can tell this by the fresh colour of the wood – avoid it. If it has been carved some time previously and the foliage colour and bud growth are strong, it is fine to buy. Remember, carved trees can add some age to your planting, but only consider them if they fit the mood you want to create. Remember, too, that not all trees need it.

Texture is also important. Look for plants that at least have maturity enough to have grown some bark. As the tree ages, the bark will improve. If you fancy a grove of slender, fine-barked trees such as elm or maple, select specimens without pruning scars. Equally, hollowed trunks can add a great deal of age and texture to a different kind of group.

The trunk shapes you will see are almost certainly going to be variations on the 'S' bend and the straighter upright forms. Try to select a number that are similar in form, because this will give an overall feeling of unity to your planting, but at the same time look for some variation in

Papaver nudicaule *'Pacino' – close-up of poppy flowerhead with a diaphonous bug.*

height and thickness, as both these factors add a lively appearance to the finished result.

Roots

Radially placed surface roots add tremendously to the look of age in each tree and lend a feeling of established permanence to the finished planting. As you search for a spread of roots (and these are often buried, so 'search' is the right word), try to find plants with roots that run in at least three different directions. They will often have more than one set of roots and a little poking around soon locates the best.

If the plant has been imported, try wiggling it gently. If there is an immediate circular cracking around the original rootball, this means that the 'pot-on' soil has not worked. Find another tree. If your wiggling reveals a sudden depression around the roots, also avoid the tree, as this means that it was carelessly potted and there is a hollow below the trunk. I once found this on a superb trident maple, where the feeder roots below the trunk had desiccated as a result. Make sure you check.

Branches

Most of the branches you see will either be wire-shaped into 'S' bends that correspond with the trunk, or clipped and grown so that they are bushy and compact. The better wired trees will have some secondary branch wiring as well. The wired branch profile is normally flattish, the clipped branch roundish in feeling. Both are acceptable as long as they work with your overview. Avoid wire-scarred plants.

Soil

If you live in a country where the soil is removed prior to importation, look for good root penetration of the new soil, discernible in well-spread new shoots and healthy foliage. In countries where a minimum of imported soil is allowed, make sure that the 'pot-on' soil is hospitable to the extending roots – this is where the trunk wiggle described above can help.

Check the soil texture. It should look open and smell sweet: plants need oxygen around their roots as well as water, and poorly drained plants smell musty. I once repotted a student's tree from an importing nursery, where the roots had grown out of the original Japanese soil, looked at the pot-on soil, made a 'U' turn and grown back. I wish I had photographed both roots and student when I discovered this! The incident was funny because we knew what to do, but without the necessary knowledge an unsuspecting buyer could have acquired this tree and had it die back constantly through bad drainage.

Native and local bonsai

Native and local trees are often a better proposition than imported specimens, as they are adapted to the local conditions and usually grow better as a result. Check the points already described.

SUITABLE TREES

Detailed cultivation advice for all the trees listed below is given in the Tree Care Directory. This features plants that are strong and attractive and should not let you down. Others will suggest themselves as you experiment with the hobby.

BEECH (European, Japanese White)

Fagus sylvatica, F. crenata

The beech is a large tree. The broad, spear-shaped leaves are retained through the winter as a bud-protection device and are shed as the new leaves unfurl; mature foliage is dark green and lustrous. The bark becomes silver-grey with age. The European beech has a number of varieties, including red- and purple-leaved forms. It can be collected, or purchased from general nurseries. The Japanese species has striking white bark and smaller leaves than the European beech. Look for Japanese beech as imported bonsai.

BOX

Buxus species

Box is a small evergreen tree or large shrub. The bark is yellowy brown and develops a pattern of small squares with age. The leaves are dense and dark brown, shiny, small and oval. Growth becomes very dense and bushy with pruning – you can sometimes see ancient box trees that have been grown and clipped in formal European gardens. There are a number of dwarf cultivars and they are all worth trying as bonsai.

CEDAR (Japanese)

Cryptomeria japonica

Cryptomeria is a large, upright-growing, evergreen tree. The leaves are dark green and pointed. Young shoot growth is bright green, and the bark darkens to brown and becomes shaggy and red-brown with age. Older trees have weeping lower branches and horizontal to upright branches in the middle to upper part. There are many varieties: some are

Accent plant: potentilla. Pot by Dan Barton. Dan has trained the yellow-flowered shrub to cascade over the stone, and he displays it on a black Chinese stand.

good, but not all care for pot culture. 'Tansu' is a reliable dwarf cultivar that has tiny features and gives a nice feeling of scale and perspective even on a 5cm (2in) plant. It is available from specialist miniature conifer outlets and as imported bonsai.

COTONEASTER

C. horizontalis and other species

Rockspray is the common name for this low-growing, flowering and fruiting deciduous shrub with an attractive arching, multi-trunk growth habit. The twigs are opposite and borne all along the branches, giving a 'herringbone' appearance. The leaves are tiny, dark green and shiny, the flowers pink and the berries bright red. Older bark is silvery buff in colour. Cotoneaster is available from most general nurseries and as a garden plant everywhere.

CYPRESS (Sawara)

Chamaecyparis pisifera

The Sawara cypress is an upright-growing, medium-sized, evergreen tree. There are many named varieties, a number of which have fan-like, curly-edged leaves, but one of the best for small landscape work is 'Tsukumo', syn. 'Tsukumo-hiba'. This is a dwarf variety that is hardy and responds very well to pruning. The leaves are dark green, curled and become very tight with soft pinching. It is available as an imported bonsai.

ELM (Chinese)

Ulmus parvifolia

The Chinese elm is a medium-sized tree that is semi-evergreen in areas with mild winters. It has dark green, lustrous, oval leaves and will produce tiny leaves when soft pruned. All features of the tree can be encouraged to reduce in size through regular pruning. The bark is dark brown to grey and becomes rough. There are many varieties: among the best are 'Corticosa', with corky bark, and 'Seiju', a small-leaved cultivar. Chinese elm is available from bonsai nurseries.

HEMLOCK (Western, Eastern)

Tsuga heterophylla, T. canadensis

The hemlock is a medium to large, upright-growing, evergreen tree. The leaves are dark green, dense and needle-like but blunt-pointed. The branches become dense, like a cedar; they are spreading and the growth is borne on arching sub-branches, giving the trees an elegant appearance. The bark is dark brown and thickens with age. In the small landscape, the hemlock resembles a true cedar but has smaller features. It may be collected, or purchased from conifer nurseries.

HORNBEAM

Carpinus betulus and other species

Like its relative the beech, the hornbeam is a medium to large, deciduous tree that retains its lance-shaped leaves through the winter. The leaves are green, and the bark thickens and matures to a silver-buff colour. Hornbeam may be collected, and some types – such as the Japanese and Korean hornbeams (Carpinus laxiflora and C. turczaninowii) – can be found as imported bonsai.

JUNIPER (Chinese)

Juniperus chinensis, J. x media

The Chinese juniper is a medium to large, evergreen tree. The dark green leaves are fine in texture, and normally cord-like with a proportion of needled growth mixed in. The bark is reddish,

Accent plant: Trifolium repens purpurescens. Pot by Phyl Barton. The cluster of wild black clover leaves looks beautiful against the lines of the stand.

becoming dark brown and stringy with age. The plant responds well to soft pruning and the growth becomes dense.

Good ones to look for among smooth-foliage forms are *Juniperus chinensis sargentii* (this is called 'Shimpaku' by some) and *J. x media* 'Blaauw', a blue-green form. Both these have largely scale-like adult foliage. These are the classical Chinese junipers seen in bonsai. If a needled (juvenile foliage) plant is wanted, choose *J.* 'Procumbens' and *J. chinensis* 'San José', both of which are tough and reliable, and greatly preferable to the needle juniper (*J. rigida*), which, although it is widely seen in bonsai, is a weak plant. Chinese junipers are available from general nurseries and as imported bonsai.

LARCH (Japanese, European)

Larix kaempferi (syn. leptolepis), L. decidua

A large deciduous, coniferous tree, the larch is upright-growing with a spreading branch habit. The branches are graceful and the numerous twigs are small and compact.

The leaves are brilliantly green in spring and they turn a light golden brown in autumn. Larch can be collected, or purchased from bonsai nurseries.

MAPLE (Japanese)

Acer palmatum

The Japanese maple is a medium-sized, deciduous tree. The leaves are small and five- to seven-lobed, with each lobe pointed and lightly toothed. Autumn colour is brilliant red. The bark is grey-buff and the twigs are red and green.

There are many varieties: you should look for small-leaved cultivars such as 'Kyohime' and 'Kashima'. These, and a number of red-leaved varieties such as 'Chishio', 'Deshojo' and 'Seigen', are a little tender, but very pretty. They can be found in general nurseries and as imported bonsai.

MAPLE (Trident)

Acer buergerianum

The trident maple is another medium-sized, deciduous tree. The leaves are small with three lobes, sharply pointed on some varieties while others are rounded. All turn a brilliant red in autumn. The bark is grey-buff and the twigs become grey-black with age. The surface rootage on trident maple is very striking. The trees can be found in general nurseries and as imported bonsai.

PINE (Scots)

Pinus sylvestris and cultivars

The Scots pine is a large, evergreen tree. The needles are dark green to blue, pointed and borne in twos. The bark is salmon-pink on the upper trunk and grey-black in the lower parts. It thickens with age into deep plates. There are many varieties – 'Beuvronensis' is probably the most common and the best one available. Scots pine can be collected, and the named varieties may be purchased from specialist conifer nurseries.

SPRUCE (Alberta)

Picea var. *glauca albertiana*

The Alberta spruce is a small to medium-sized, evergreen shrub. The needles are small, dark green, pointed and dense. The bark is dark brown and thickens with age. A dwarf variety that is very effective in a miniature landscape, specimens can be found in general nurseries and as bonsai.

YEW (English)

Taxus baccata

The English yew is an evergreen that makes a tree of massive growth and branch spread, and it lives to a great age. The leaves are flatly needled and a deep, glossy green. The bark is deep red-grey and it becomes fissured with age. The female plants bear bright red fruit. English yew can be collected, and it can be purchased from conifer and general nurseries.

ACCENT PLANTS

As the name suggests, 'accent plants' are displayed as companions to the main planting. They are much smaller than the planting they accompany, but their contribution can work on the emotions of the viewer very effectively. This is made possible by the simplicity of the plant material and the rustic feeling of the wonderfully expressive pots used, as well as by the texture, colour and mood of the individual accent plants chosen to counterpoint the main landscape.

The colours of the flowers and foliage, and the texture, form and colours of the containers combine to make the selection, growing and appreciation of accent plants a delightful extension to the making of a miniature landscape – and a fascinating hobby in its own right. The search for these plants will give you a lot of pleasure and will make you look at plants in a new way: even a sunflower or a dandelion planted in a tiny pot can be enough to set a mood, and yes, they do miniaturize (my wife Kate tells the story of how on one occasion her single tiny sunflower stole the show right from under the noses of those huge display bonsai – and the public loved it!). All you have to do is to take a tiny pot and sow the seed directly into it, and both the plant and its flower will remain small.

There are many images of accent plants throughout the book for you to enjoy, and suitable species from which to choose are listed below.

SUITABLE ACCENT PLANTS

Acorus varieties
Ajuga reptans 'Atropurpurea' (Purple-leaved bugle)
Arthropodium candidum (Turk lily)
Arundinaria pygmaea (Dwarf bamboo)
Briza maxima (Quaking grass)
Chamaemelum nobile 'Treneague' (Lawn chamomile)
Corydalis varieties
Deschampsia flexuosa 'Tatra Gold' (Golden grass)
Dianthus varieties (Cottage pinks)
Equisetum varieties (Water horsetail)
Ferns, small
Festuca varieties
Hakonechloa macra 'Aureola'
Hebe 'James Stirling', *H. pimeloides* 'Quicksilver'
Imperata cylindrica (Blood grass)
Iris varieties, dwarf
Juncus varieties (Indian reed)
Leontopodium alpinum 'Mignon' (Edelweiss)

Ophiopogon planiscapus nigrescens (Black mondo grass)
Oxalis acetosella (Wood sorrel)
Oxalis magellanica 'Nelson' (Dwarf shamrock)
Parachetus communis (Shamrock pea)
Parahebe catarractae 'Porlock Purple'
Pieris japonica 'Little Heath' (Dwarf andromeda)
Polygonum varieties (Knotweed)
Pratia pedunculata
Reeds, small
Saxifraga varieties
Scutellaria varieties (Skullcap)
Sedum varieties
Sempervivum varieties (Houseleek)
Sisyrinchium varieties
Spiraea japonica varieties
Spiraea thunbergii
Thymus varieties (Thyme)
Viola labradorica (Purple-leaved violet)

CHAPTER FOUR

shaping
the plants

The easiest way to control, shape and maintain your planting is by the use of established bonsai techniques. These are traditional methods that have been used in China and Japan for centuries, and they enable you to keep everything within bounds and looking really healthy without unduly stressing either plant or owner! Today these methods have moved around the world and some new ways of shaping plants have evolved that are adapted to the local situation. As this happens, an international east-west language of plant styling is emerging.

BASIC BONSAI TECHNIQUES

Removing the Tap Root

In nature, a tree has a major tap root that ties it firmly into the ground, along with many flanking radial roots that spread from the surface down and underneath the tree – like a reverse image of the branch profile below ground. In bonsai, the tap root is removed, as are any other heavy roots, and these will then be replaced with a copious growth of fine feeding roots. With the removal of

Removing the tap root

1. By removing the tap root and other lower anchor roots, the root system is encouraged to become fibrous.

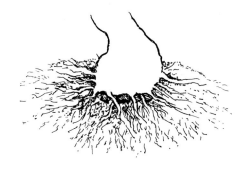

2. The roots under the trunk are made active and the tree undergoes a consolidation of strength. This compact root activity keeps the transfer of nutrition and the metabolism at youthful levels and the tree responds well to training schedules.

the tap root, root activity is transferred back under the trunk and the finer root pad enables the tree to grow happily within the limits of a small pot. (This is where the name comes from: 'bonsai' means 'tree in a tray', or something similar.)

The Pot and Root Pruning

The pot in which a bonsai is grown acts as a flowerpot and picture frame combined. It must therefore have display value and also function perfectly as a growing vehicle. This means that the shape must suit the planting and the pot must drain well, so it needs ample drainage holes in order to shed excess water – the roots are confined for a long time and must enjoy a good water/oxygen exchange.

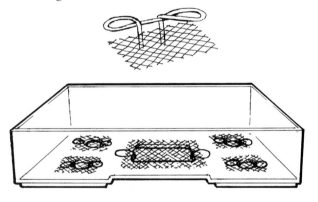

The pot
The bonsai pot acts as both flowerpot and picture frame. Drainage holes must be ample and work efficiently, as there must never be stagnant water. 'Butterflies' are formed with wire to locate the drainage mesh as shown. The wire 'legs' are passed through and the loops above and ends beneath the pot are bent sideways, securing the mesh firmly.

The root activity of a bonsai so confined slows down, and as the roots fill the container a tidier type of top growth ensues.

After a year or two, according to age and species, the plant becomes pot-bound and it is repotted when all the available soil has been utilized. The tree is taken out of the container and a third of the old soil is removed. Half the exposed

Root pruning

1. *Root pruning is carried out in stages. First, remove the tree from the pot and wash away the outer third of the old soil.*

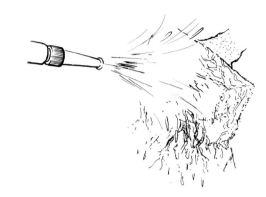

2. *Next, comb out the roots.*

3. *Prune one half of the exposed root length. In addition, make sure that surface roots remain surfaced – more may be located and added. Older and heavier lower roots are pruned to encourage finer ones.*

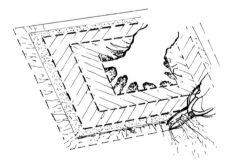

4. *Finally, even out the whole root mass by pruning to balance the spread of roots.*

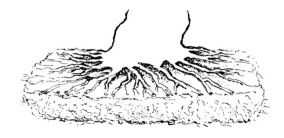

root length is pruned away, particularly the old lower roots, to encourage the production of new feeder roots. The upper, surfaced roots are part of the design and are not pruned – they add an important aged quality to the trunk and the image you are creating. The tree is then replanted in the same pot. Sometimes a cosmetic change may be made to another one that better suits the emerging shape, but a bonsai is never potted on like other plants. The idea is to keep growth compact and the plant operating in a restricted environment.

There are aesthetic considerations regarding placement in the pot, angle and so on, and I have made reference to these in Chapter 1, where the featured miniature landscapes are described, and in the project instructions given in Chapter 7.

Soil

The soil used for bonsai must be open and free draining. There are many mixes, so use what works for you (for components, see page 38). The best soils are often based on sands. Knowledgeable gardeners have used sandy composts to root plants for hundreds of years: it also makes sense to use sandy soil for bonsai because there is little deterioration in such mixes and the plants must stay in the same soil, often for years at a stretch.

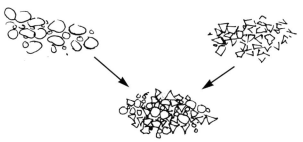

Soil

The key factors in soil for bonsai are open texture, particle size and degree of roughness. Sieve out the ultra-fine sand (this can be used later for contouring the soil). Use sand particles of pinhead to match-head size in a 50/50 combination of sharp and rounded particles. Such a soil makes for strong roots.

Root tips hitting sharp sand tend to divide and this produces an echoing division in the top growth of the tree.

Trunk and Branch Shaping

The trunk and branches of a bonsai are pruned to maintain a balance with the modified, smaller root system. This neatens the branches, inducing taper and giving characterful changes of direction to the expanding growth. Twig size is also reduced by pruning and a sense of miniature scale is soon produced. The shape of the trunk and branches can be further modified by coiling them with wire and bending them into a new form. Properly done, wiring is a fascinating process that completely transforms the humblest small plant.

The trick when applying wire is to use soft aluminium training wire specially made for the job, and to select a thickness that will bend the wood without buckling it. For most small trees, 1–3mm gauge wire is ideal. The process of wiring consists of coiling the wire around the trunk, branches and twigs and bending them into a pleasantly unified shape. There are, of course, many combinations of shapes and a number of examples are shown in this chapter. I have also illustrated coiling and locking the wire by moving from branch to branch via the trunk (see page 62).

When wiring a tree, the two key things to remember are not to coil too tight – the plant expands as it grows and gets wire-scarred before you know it – and thereafter to check for wire tightness once a week. If the wire appears tight, it should be removed immediately.

3. *Sometimes the trunk may be grown on and cut back several times, allowing at least two or three years of free growth between cuts. This creates a surprisingly natural taper and helps to shape the tree. Trunks may also be trained by wire coiling alone, or by a combination of these techniques.*

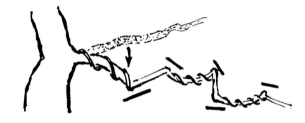

Trunk and branch shaping

1. *Trunk pruning is the answering technique to root pruning. The growth energy is redirected back into the plant and an explosion of vigour is produced.*

4. *Branches are formed by wiring them into position, pruning soft growth and by trimming them back regularly. This maintains them and builds character as growth is forced to change direction.*

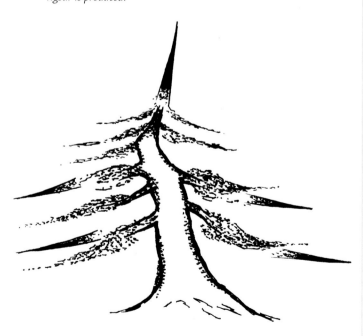

5. *The key is to match the form and flow of the trunk and branches.*

Accent plant: Phalaris arundinaria, a white-striped grass. Pot by Dan Barton. The silver blades of the grass look wonderful in the blue-grey pot.

2. *The trunk puts out many branches as the energy surges through it.*

Do not try to back-coil the wire as this often leads to branch breakages: just cut it off using wire cutters that cut right to the tips of their blades. The Japanese pattern are made for the job – they offer good leverage and are well worth the investment.

When trees need their trunks thickening, they can be planted in a large box or garden bed, fed and watered freely, and allowed to grow and expand roots and top growth – the trunks will thicken at a great rate.

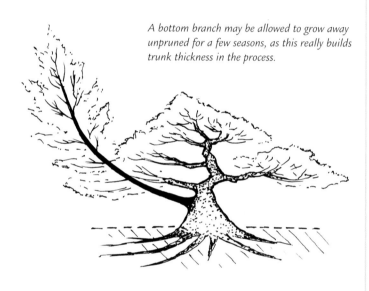

A bottom branch may be allowed to grow away unpruned for a few seasons, as this really builds trunk thickness in the process.

Once its job is done, the branch is removed and can then be carved as a decorative snag.

Ageing

The process of making your small plant look like an old-timer is fascinating and involves a number of steps.

Trunk angle

A more or less vertical trunk is characteristic of a young tree.

Planting the tree with its trunk at an angle adds an instant feeling of age.

The first consideration is **trunk angle**. In most cases a trunk will look older when planted at a slight angle rather than with the 'straight up in the air' look of the young tree. The formal upright tree and the broom style (see pages 61 and 63) are the exceptions: the ageing of these styles is reinforced by careful placement of their surface roots.

The exceptions are formal upright and broom style trees, where age is reinforced by the arrangement of their surface roots.

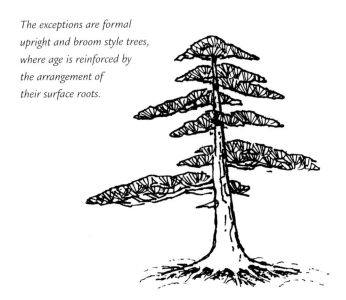

Surface roots are important in giving the trunk an aged look. Suitable roots can be located and surfaced at root-pruning time – usually they are made from the roots you encounter first as you feel around the base of the trunk. When raised so that they radiate from the base of the trunk, these roots will add a tremendous feeling of age to a small tree. Such roots are usually quite easy to place when they are young.

Bark texture is another factor in creating an aged appearance, so be careful to grow and display the tree so that its best texture is emphasized.

If possible, choose trunks with acceptable **taper**, as this adds yet another dimension to the illusion of great age. Alternatively, build taper by the cut-and-grow method (see page 56).

Where **carving** is involved, make sure it remains a quiet element, no matter how extensive. You can do this by carving with the grain using a thin, circular wire brush fixed in a router, which will give a natural kind of grooving. A lot of contour blending can be achieved with sympathetic carving.

When carving, make it deep enough to cast a shadow. Very often the wood 'furs' and looks fuzzy-edged. This is because it is wet – allow a month or two for it to dry and it will then cut as sweetly as sharpening a pencil.

The last stage of the carving itself involves following the original grooving with a finer cutter to add detail and the effect of the natural grain. Never over-model your carving, because this looks very artificial, and be careful to avoid such clichés as the woodpecker hole!

Ageing techniques
The tree shown here demonstrates a number of ageing techniques: surface roots; trunk taper; carving; silvering; branch angles. The whole tree has been grown to display its best texture, the mature and fissured bark reinforcing the feeling of age.

The final element lies in colouring and preserving the wood, known as **silvering**. Lime sulphur is used to preserve and whiten the carved area so that it resembles old dead wood. I add a further dimension to soften the whiteness of dried lime sulphur by tinting the carved wood with grey watercolour: I use designers' gouache in mid-grey and heighten it with black, making sure it gets into the recesses. This creates 'depth' and visually models the carving. You can either pre-tint the wood before treating with lime sulphur, or apply the colour on top after drying. This 'ages' the carving nicely. When redundant branches are pruned, keep them as carved and treated shortened snags so that they add age to the tree.

Branch angles are also important in giving an appearance of age. Most branches should be wired and trained to flow down and then up towards their terminals, as old branches generally weep in this way.

Detail of branch angle
Most old branches weep down and then up towards their ends, so aim to reproduce this form when wiring.

Branch pruning with the cut-and-grow method (see page 56) can be used to create taper and character.

On the **soil surface**, spread peat and topsoil mixed to a paste with water, and then press fine-textured sheet moss into it. If you concentrate on placing the moss between the surface roots and confine it largely to the trunk base area, a pleasing illusion of settled age can be created.

You can have a lot of fun using these, and other techniques that will flow from them as you work, to make your landscapes appear really well established and very old.

MAINTENANCE

There are three important factors involved in maintaining a bonsai planting in good condition.

Watering

This is a key factor. Bonsai need constant moisture, and this is particularly important for the small-sized trees used in miniature landscapes. From spring to autumn, when the trees are in active growth, the soil will need to be kept moist. In winter, during dormancy, it is enough to keep it damp.

Feeding

Bonsai need fertilizer to give them nutrition in a soil that soon has all available food leached out of it by the constant watering required by the trees. Regular feeding from spring to autumn will take care of most of their needs. A well-balanced plant food such as Miracle-Gro should be given twice a month and the cycle finished off with late-season feeds of 0–10–10 to harden the growth.

Placement

Placement is the third key factor. Bonsai and miniature landscapes are so pretty that the urge to grow them inside the house is tremendous, but sadly, most of the species used cannot tolerate indoor conditions. There are indoor species that may be used, but growing these often involves special care, growing lights and temperature control. Instead, the tree species generally used are grown outside and brought indoors for limited display periods only. Keen growers often display their plants on outdoor elevated shelves so that they can be seen and enjoyed from the house. They may then be brought inside for *short* spells only – perhaps just a day. Most bonsai and miniature landscapes will need frost protection in winter to avoid damage to branches, twigs and so on.

STYLING

The following pages give details of the various forms in which bonsai are styled, and then looks at the different ways in which they can be planted in groups to create a miniature landscape.

Formal

An upright form is the most common of all the trunk forms used in miniature landscapes. In individual bonsai it is often treated very formally, with branches occurring no lower than one-third of the way up the trunk. The first branch is placed to either left or right, with the next step up in reverse placement, the third to the rear and so on. In the miniature landscape, however, this style will look better treated less formally.

Ideally, the trunk should be upright and feature surface roots, but even this may be relaxed in landscape work, which uses a lot of ground cover of different types (including plants, sand and rocks – see page 77–79). Branches can follow an alternating placement pattern, with some at the back to give depth. They should diminish in size and complexity from the bottom to the top of the trunk. The apex can be treated in different ways, but often looks best kept small as a simplified cone of foliage.

In this style, branches are usually broadly wedge-shaped in plan and shallowly triangular in profile, tapering to pointed terminals. The main branches should be straightish, in harmony with the trunk.

Formal style
1. *The trunk is wired and straightened to a pleasing form. You do not have to be too devoted to a rigid line – in landscapes it is better to go for a natural feeling. The branches are wired into position and can be placed in threes (left, right and back), varying the radial placement so that branches do not shade each other out.*

2. *Branch planes are wedge-shaped, tapering towards the terminal.*

3. *Foliage profiles are shallow and kept compact with careful pinching. To avoid the look of topiary, try not to be mechanical when doing this.*

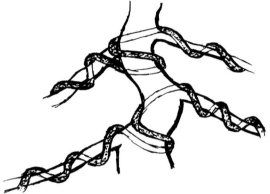

4. *This detail shows how wires should be placed for maximum leverage and neatness.*

5. *The trunk/branch junctions are opened up to enhance the feeling of age and define the structure.*

6. *Surface roots are placed radially as far as possible, although they are often hidden as the landscape develops. As the tree is being potted, you can physically spread and position the roots for the best effect. Ensure that they enter the soil gradually, as the effect is lost if they suddenly head downwards in a nose dive!*

Broom

The broom shape arose from observation of the natural form of deciduous species such as the elms, where the trunk is upright and the branches sweep upwards. The image presented by a good broom style bonsai or landscape planting, particularly in winter, is what everyone thinks of as a 'real tree'.

The form is upright, sometimes tall and tapered with the branches rising from different heights along the trunk, and sometimes short and squat with most of the branch activity confined to the upper parts of the trunk. There are countless variations in between. The branch pattern varies with each design, but normally is developed as a wide tapered fan with an elegant periphery of twigs. A well-spread surface root formation is regarded as a bonus in this style, as it adds so much to the natural feeling of an old tree.

3. *The twigs are thinned to create 'negative windows' along the branches, paying particular attention as the tree matures to the areas around branch/trunk junctions. If these are cleaned out, the opened branch structure will 'age' the image.*

4. *Trimming back in autumn keeps the inner portions of the branches budding actively.*

Broom style
1. *The trunk is wired if necessary to straighten it, and the branches are wired if required to reinforce the upward swing.*

5. *When the tree is in the formative stages, the branches may be bundled loosely together over the winter to help build the typical 'reversed umbrella' shape.*

2. *Soft pinching of new growth and periodic trimming increases the number of fine twigs and branches.*

6. *Surface roots are placed radially and carefully maintained. They are lifted and arranged at repotting time and then covered again with a pad of wet moss, as if they are kept moist they will carry on thickening.*

Informal

This is the other main tree form used in landscape work. Again, it is upright, but the informal tree is often trained to have at least one 'S' bend in the trunk, and these curves should be slow and natural rather than exaggerated. The branches are trained to spring from outer curves on the trunk with an alternating placement, and a number are directed to the rear for depth. The same tapering of size and complexity as in the formal tree is usual. The apex of informal trees can vary quite considerably in size as long as it remains smaller than the branches below. Branch forms follow the formal tree in principle but are softer and more rounded. As the branch line springs from the trunk, it bends down and then upwards in a slow arc. Side branches follow the same lines. The effect of several informal trees planted together is wholly natural and grove-like.

Informal style
1. *The trunk is wired into a loosely spiralled 'S' form.*

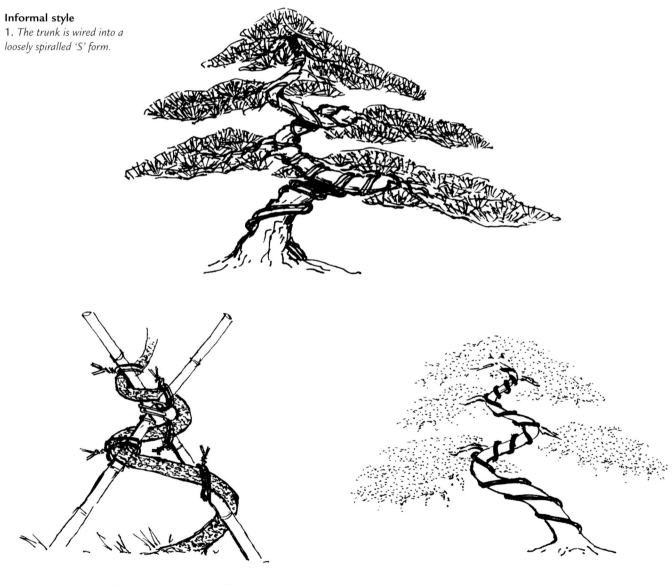

2. *Sometimes taller trunks are trained around an 'X' former made from stakes.*

3. *As the trunk is wired, the repeated curves in the upper trunk are made smaller than the lower ones.*

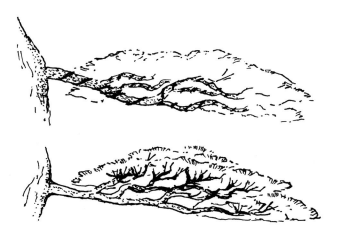

4. *In addition, the trunk is brought forward from the centre point so that the top inclines slightly to the front. This creates greater depth from front to back and a more interesting plant. This is the side view.*

5. *The branches are also wired in soft spirals and arranged so that the twigs form shaped profiles.*

6. *The branches may be wedge-shaped in plan.*

7. *The branch profiles are shallow-domed and elegant.*

8. *Alternate branching to the left, right and back is followed, but not too stringently — the effect must be natural.*

9. *This bird's-eye view shows how varied radial placement avoids overshadowing by overlapping dense branch planes.*

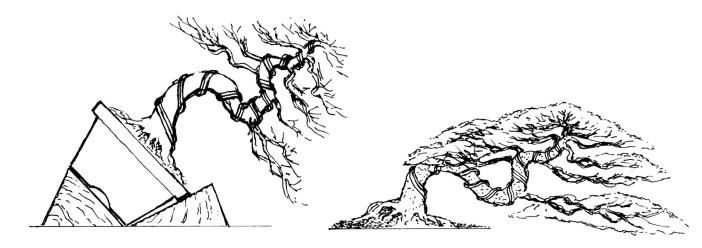

Leaning style

1. *The trunk is wired into the spiralled 'S' form used in the informal shape and then the branches are wired and spiralled. The pot is propped so that the tree stands at the chosen angle.*

2. *The branches are then bent and placed so that they reaffirm the dynamic of the trunk: those on the upper side are moved in towards the trunk line and those on the lower side are moved outwards so that they jut.*

Leaning

This tree can be curved or straight in form – the style is named from the planting angle. Branch form and placement follow the informal style. With all three styles – formal, informal and leaning – the branch angles can add a great deal of character and mood to the tree. Surface roots add a lot to this design, particularly those on the 'upper' side of the trunk as they visually and physically support the trunk, suggesting a balancing force without which the tree would collapse. This kind of shape is effective in coastal scenes.

Groups

The group is central to the whole landscape planting idea and 'works' through the image conveyed by many trunks planted together. This image can be of a tall group seen close to, or of a tiny one seen at a huge implied distance. There are thicks and thins to consider, in terms of both trunk thicknesses and the spacing in between – the negative areas are just as important to the interest of the group as are the densities of the trunk lines.

Groups

1. *The trees are chosen so that they blend together for overall form. Individual trunks can be wired and pruned for shape correction and variety, as uniformity looks dull. Choose thick and thin, tall and short. Work on the branches with wiring and pruning, so that the trees are essentially pre-styled. The number and weight of the branches controls trunk thickness and big trees will have more than little ones.*

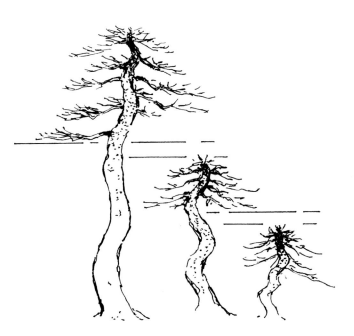

2. Groups usually have two or three major trees, and the branch pattern on these normally starts about halfway up the trunk, so that it clears the lesser trees.

3. Groups need shorter trees with lower branches at the back for added perspective. Trees planted around the major ones supply the 'left and right' tiers of branches.

The varying heights of the canopy and how it divides gives further interest to the planting.

The massed form must be unified, and when it is, a wonderfully natural feeling results. So, whatever you choose by way of shapes to portray your image, remember 'theme and variation' and it will work just that bit better for you. When assembling the group, follow the diagram sequence carefully – the technique really is simple and very effective.

Note that the grid is always removed at the first repot, but before that keep an eye on the tie wires and cut them if they are biting into the roots.

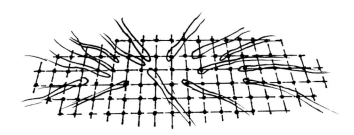

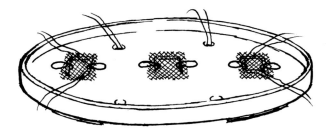

Assembling a group

1. *Securing the trunks in their chosen relationship is the key to setting up a good group. I use a grid because I like positive control when the design is put together. The rootballs are tied to the grid and this 'locks' the trees into position. This system is better for them as it prevents lateral movement, and immobilized trees grow good roots. The grid can be made from garden canes tied together, heavy wires or a plastic lattice-based plant tray. Secure plenty of location wires to the grid and drape them flat, out of the way.*

2. Prepare the pot with plastic mesh over the drainage holes. Secure these with wire 'butterflies' to lock them in place. Add location wires, passing them through the drainage holes and the smaller holes made specially for them, and drape them over the pot rim.

3. *Add a drainage course of coarse sand and place some sieved soil mix over it.*

4. *Unpot the trees, spread their roots and trim as necessary. Arrange the trees on the grid according to your plan and tie the root systems to the mesh by twist-tying the location wires over them.*

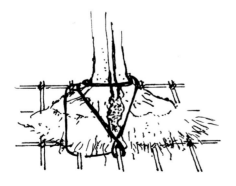

5. *Trunks that need closer proximity can have their roots sliced to make them fit and are then tied together and twist-tied.*

Opposite: Accent plant: Carex cultivar, a yellow grass. Pot by Dan Barton. Combined with the natural bowl form and the bamboo mat, the grass suggests a tranquil garden corner or the margin of a pond.

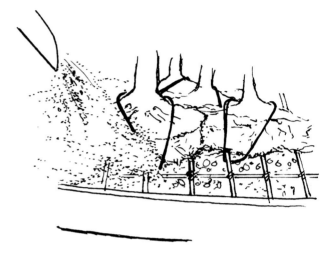

6. *Add more soil and make certain this permeates every face of the roots and passes through the grid.*

7. *Work on the surface roots to lift and feature them. Consider the planting at a distance and adjust the branch planes by bending and pruning. Deeper detailing comes later, once the group is prospering. Mound the soil to make hills and promontories as desired, then water everything with a fine spray. Add moss, pressing it down and making sure the edges sit down. Water again until the excess drips from the holes.*

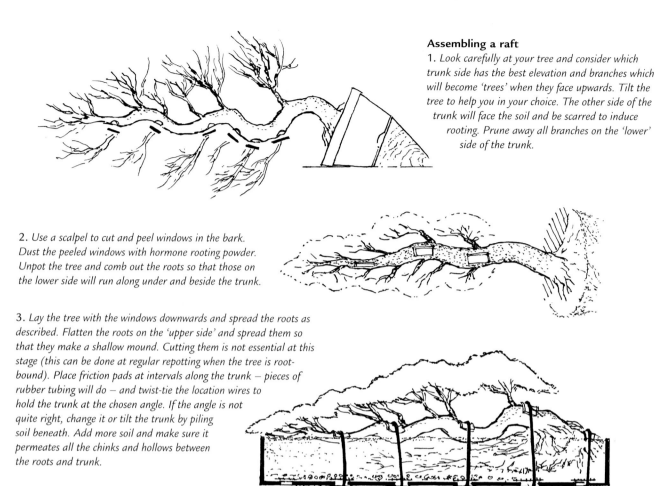

Assembling a raft
1. *Look carefully at your tree and consider which trunk side has the best elevation and branches which will become 'trees' when they face upwards. Tilt the tree to help you in your choice. The other side of the trunk will face the soil and be scarred to induce rooting. Prune away all branches on the 'lower' side of the trunk.*

2. *Use a scalpel to cut and peel windows in the bark. Dust the peeled windows with hormone rooting powder. Unpot the tree and comb out the roots so that those on the lower side will run along under and beside the trunk.*

3. *Lay the tree with the windows downwards and spread the roots as described. Flatten the roots on the 'upper side' and spread them so that they make a shallow mound. Cutting them is not essential at this stage (this can be done at regular repotting when the tree is root-bound). Place friction pads at intervals along the trunk – pieces of rubber tubing will do – and twist-tie the location wires to hold the trunk at the chosen angle. If the angle is not quite right, change it or tilt the trunk by piling soil beneath. Add more soil and make sure it permeates all the chinks and hollows between the roots and trunk.*

Raft

This is a variation on the group where a whole tree is laid down and the branches become 'trunks'. It is a fascinating process and an easy one to do. Once the recumbent mother trunk has generated roots along its length, the parent root mass is removed and the whole planting is transferred into a shallow pot. Then long-term training of the new branch/trunk lines can be carried out. The pot acts as a picture frame at this point and enables you to focus on the branch/trunk structure in relation to the base line of the old trunk.

When starting a raft-style planting, give some thought to the form of the recumbent trunk – the actual process of inducing roots is easy. Imagine how your planting will look with either an undulating or a straight-line base and pick a tree that suits your mental picture – some thought at this stage pays dividends in future quality.

You will need to prepare a container long enough to take the length of the tree when you lay it down. Place drainage mesh over the holes and secure them with butterflies. Pass location wires up through the drainage holes and drape the ends over the edge of the pot (see diagrams for assembling a group). Add drainage sand and bottom soil. Now follow the steps shown in the diagrams.

When you have completed the assembly, water in well and shade the tree: roots should appear within a month or two. Styling of the branches/trees is best confined to pruning until the roots are well formed – this will take about a year – as undue movement of the trunk through wiring may break emerging root tips.

Root Connected

Similar to the raft, this variation differs from it in that the old trunk is suppressed and side shoots are trained outwards along the soil, become rooted and then grow up. The planting is then styled as a group with a very interesting diverse base formed from all the maturing original side shoots. Both this and the raft are based on trees suffering natural damage and surviving through realigning their growth.

The root-connected tree can be started by hard-pruning the trunk of a freely suckering species such as elm. Many buds will be thrown out from the base and the surface root line. Allow these to develop freely and then scar them, dust the peeled area with hormone rooting powder and peg them down to induce rooting. A whole web of rooted, connected bases and emerging shoots/trunks will appear. An alternative method is shown in the diagram. With either method, make sure you transplant the tree into a pot big enough for the roots to grow freely.

Creating a root-connected tree

1. *One way of starting a root-connected tree is to hard-prune the trunk above a whorl of branches and layer the trunk beneath them.*

2. *The whorled branches are wired out sideways and the trunk is layered to produce roots close beneath the branches. For full details of how to do this, see Project 10 on page 108.*

DEVELOPING YOUR STYLE

The bonsai styles I have discussed are those on which the miniature landscape is largely based, and you can use any of these arrangements as a basis for creating something really personal. The styles themselves are based on observations of natural tree forms: they are an attempt to reproduce the core and essence of what was seen and it is helpful to draw on them in order to get your ideas flowing.

You will soon want to interpret nature in your own way, and the various bonsai exhibition annuals from Japan are treasure houses of ideas. You will note that few exhibition trees follow the styles! Take the essence of the styles, but never be too strict in following the guidelines – they should be thought of as a beginning, never as an end in themselves.

3. *The rooted layer is planted in a wide pot and the branches are scarred and pegged down to root as well.*

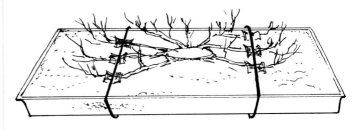

4. *When the new trunks have grown to 30cm (12in) they are cut back by half, and this produces many lateral buds for branching. The trunks can be wired at this time. Regrow the trunk lines and trim them back twice a year, and you will soon have a really interesting plant.*

making the landscape

In this chapter we look in detail at how the miniature landscape is put together, using the design of a grove of trees on a low cape overlooking the sea as the example. The finished landscape shown here was given to the Pacific Rim Bonsai Collection.

Bill Jordan and I worked as a team in producing the assembly in front of the camera, after which I sketched pictures and wrote captions for ten probable pictures.

When Bill returned to England and saw the photographic results, he suggested extending the sequence to 20 photographs to tell a complete story. I agreed, and wrote the text and captions as I remembered things happening, in order to share as closely as possible the atmosphere of an actual 'work in progress' with you.

We gave a lot of thought as to how to make the project clear, fun and vivid. We decided against a studio environment in order to keep the feeling of genuine back-garden situations. We also hoped you might enjoy the problem-solving approach. Bill's bonsai knowledge enables him to take informed photographs that help to clarify how everything is assembled and the landscape carefully created.

COMPONENTS

Five *Cryptomeria japonica* 'Tansu' Height: 30cm (12in). Source: bonsai nursery stock, about six years old from cuttings. 'Tansu' is compact rather than slow growing and makes good, dense branches.

Training wire Aluminium, 1.5mm and 2mm gauges.

Tools and sundries Trimming shears in two sizes, branch pruners, rake, wire cutters.

Container Fine-quality Japanese oval pot in unglazed dark brown clay, from the Yamaki kiln. Size: 52.5 x 37.5 x 5cm (21 x 15 x 2in). Donated by David Degroot.

Location grid Cannibalized from the open-mesh base of a plastic growing tray.

Soil Fine red pumice, bark and grit. This came from the potting shed at the Pacific Rim Bonsai Collection, the idea being that the finished planting could then be watered in the same manner as the other bonsai in the collection. I recycled some of the old soil from the cryptomerias and mixed it in.

'Cape' stone Warm grey, landscape-shaped stone in which the form resembles a low cliff. Size: 30 x 10 x 7.5cm (12 x 4 x 3in). Collected in Wales 25 years ago.

Sand Fine grey, to suggest water.

Mosses Low growing.

METHOD

The cryptomerias were bushy and well grown. I purchased them from a friend in early autumn and fed and watered them well until the time of assembling the planting early the following summer.

The original trees.

The first step was to take the plants out of their pots. The soil surface was cleaned and raked away enough to show the trunk base. Branches and the branch/trunk junctions were cleaned of inner and dangling foliage. They were then wired and shaped. This involved pruning and thinning foliage to open it up enough to feature individual branch lines. After bending, the branches were pruned for length and to detail the profiles. They were then put back into their pots to keep the roots moist.

After styling.

After styling, the trees assumed individual character, but still largely preserved the image of the species – that is to say, nothing was too curved and branch length diminished towards the top of the tree. It became obvious that the plants were way too big for the project, so their height was reduced almost by half. They were then thinned again to suit their new proportions, and the branches were trimmed and rearranged for length and position.

After height reduction, thinning and further styling.

Next the plants were removed from their pots and their roots were gently combed out. They were then placed roughly in position in the container. I checked each one to see how it looked and whether it sat well next to its neighbour.

Preliminary positioning of the trees.

Root pruning.

Having ascertained how much to take off, the trees were root-pruned and the root mass of each one was reduced enough to be fitted to its neighbour. This sounds drastic! In fact, it simply meant shaving extra from the sides of some of the root masses so that the trunks might come close together here and there. The trees were then shaded and the old damp soil was heaped over their roots. When you make a planting, it is vital always to keep the roots damp as you work.

I now realized that I had not prepared the planting location grid, so I grabbed a plastic plant tray with a mesh base and cannibalized a chunk of that. I cut through the mesh with scissors and to my delight the grid was strong but flexible – just right! The grid was carefully shaped to the contour of the oval pot using scissors.

Preparing the location grid.

Test positioning the trees.

Twist-tying the trees to the grid.

Next I passed tie wires through the mesh and began to place the trees roughly, twist-tying them loosely into test positions. The trees were carefully rotated for the best aspect. In a landscape they have to work together, so this selection process is a little different to the usual one in bonsai, where you only have to worry about the best aspects of a single trunk. Compensation for that lies in the way the combined branch lines give instantly satisfying 'landscape' effects – you get a nice sweep of green early on.

After satisfying myself about their positions, more ties were added until the trees stood easily on the grid. The trick is not to use so much pressure that the roots are constricted, but to use enough so that they stand without toppling. Next I tried the arrangement in the container to get an idea of how things were going. So far it looked pretty good.

The soil was mixed from the brighter new blend of red pumice, bark and grit, combined with the recycled soil from the cryptomerias, which is the

Finding the best aspect.

All the trees fixed in position on the grid.

Above: *Trying the arrangement in the container.*

darker soil in the picture. This, too, included quite a lot of grit.

It is a good idea to retain an element of the old soil, as this contains beneficial micro-organisms that help the trees to settle in quickly, smoothing out transplant shock that can be aggravated with a total change of soil.

I had enjoyed the cape stone as a separate viewing stone for many years, but its size seemed perfect for the landscape and the 'right' elements should always be used without worrying about any other considerations. Only by investing in your concept to the best of your ability, whether it be in terms of time, effort or sometimes money, can you hope to get the very best out of it.

Above right: *The soil components, including some of the trees' original soil.*

Below right: *The cape stone.*

First the drainage mesh was secured with location wires to hold it lightly in place. The soils were then mixed together and sieved to lose the heavier particles and the fines – I kept the fines for contouring the soil later. A layer of soil was then placed in the container and the 'grid-locked' group was tried for fit in the container – all was fine, except that the grid would not clear the back of the stone when I tried to place it. The solution was to shave a bit off the grid and pack soil so that it flowed up the back of the stone. The grid then sat on top behind the stone and was wired to hold it in position. The stone was bedded into the base soil, then more soil was added in and around the

Above right: *Side view, with the trees in position on top of the mounded soil and against the stone. This view shows the significant front-to-back depth of the arrangement.*

Right: *Ensuring soil penetration.*

Below: *Adjusting the contours of the trees.*

planting so that every face of the roots was covered. I used my fingers and a little probing to ensure soil penetration. Everything was then watered in using a fine spray, making sure there was enough for the surplus to drip through the drainage holes.

Then, at last, it was time to sort out the trees! I aimed for a natural mood in the planting and concentrated on adjusting contours so that they worked together, either by bending or by pruning – what a fascinating process. You really are image-making at this point.

The next stage was to build the contours around the trees and to add sheets of moss. The moss had been liberated the day before from a tree planted in the same soil mix, so I knew it would transplant well. The moss was saturated with water, drained and placed, taking care to bed in the edges well. Indentations were introduced between the moss sheets to add interest to the surface.

Above: *Adding the moss.*

Below: *Adding the fine sand.*

The fine grey sand was added last, using a teaspoon, and was carefully spread and flattened with the fingers together. Then it was time to water lightly and place the landscape in dappled shade. The whole process took about two hours from start to finish.

AFTERCARE

Provision of 30–40 per cent shade, foliage misting and careful attention to soil dampness are the main considerations.

I usually seal all pruning cuts wider than matchstick thickness: cryptomerias appreciate being turgid and pruning cuts are potential areas of desiccation, so this is important.

Moss cover can be a problem in that it masks the soil condition, absorbs water intended for lower down around the roots and hogs feed intended for the trees. Remember this, and include some removable moss flaps to enable you to check on things accurately by eye and touch. In climates with wet winters, if the trees are going to be left outside you should remove an outer band of moss inside the pot rim that is wide enough to give good air exchange, otherwise the moss will hold in too much moisture, leading to root rot. Better still, do not chance it but provide polythene sheeting to ward off the rain.

As a result of all the styling carried out as the planting was assembled, there will be some yellowing and browning of growth tips and terminal foliage. Do not worry unduly, as this is what cryptomerias do when they are pruned in this way. As the tissue dries up it can be rubbed away and picked off with the fingers. New green growth will soon bud out and cover everything.

Maintenance pruning, which involves pruning soft growth with the fingertips, does not cause browning when confined to soft green growth. Branch pruning, confined to cutting tissue with brown bark, will not cause browning of soft green growth tips.

Feed the trees with Miracle-Gro one month after planting, if the trees are obviously flourishing. If, on the other hand, growth appears slow, do not feed but carry on misting the leaves, keep the soil damp and keep the planting shaded – it will come back.

The 'final' landscape – for now.

CHAPTER SIX

making a
rock planter

I first became aware of 'ciment fondu' when I was
at art school. There it was used for sealing up the
bricked-in kiln aperture prior to firing, and I
noticed that it dried to a nice dark grey colour. In
fact, ciment fondu is an aluminous cement long
used by sculptors. I first worked with it in the
1960s, when a friend and I became heavily
involved in making Japanese 'stone' lanterns for a
series of Japanese gardens we had constructed. It
dried to a remarkably stone-like texture and
colour when mixed with the right sand and could
be hand-tooled to a chiselled finish just as old
stone lanterns would be. These cast lanterns were
probably as heavy as their granite counterparts!

After that, I worked very little with ciment
fondu, except for using it to make garden rocks
for various landscape jobs, until Bill Jordan and I

made a couple of rocks using his ciment fondu
and fibre-glass mixed technique. I liked the results
so much that I made a series of rock planters.
Mine were typical painters' creations – concerned
with design, colour and textural finish. Bill's were
more sculptural, built with fibre-glass cloth and
coats of ciment fondu over a sound structural
base and finished in a very convincing and attractive way. With typical generosity, Bill readily
agreed to my reproducing his step-by-step method
here. The photographs are of projects that Bill
worked on during a series of demonstrations he
gave while in the US.

The first thing to do is to sketch out some ideas
so that you get a feel for the size, shape and texture
of the rock you wish to create. When that is more
or less settled, assemble the various components.

YOU WILL NEED

Wood, heavy-gauge wire and scrap metal To make the armature forming the core of the sculpture.

Chicken wire Wire netting.

Fibre-glass cloth

Ciment fondu powder

Tools Scissors, wire-cutters, pliers, old paint brushes, and a selection of different trowels for mixing and modelling the cement.

Wet cloths and polythene sheeting For wrapping the wet cement.

Convenient waist-high stand For working on the rock sculpture.

Crumpled fibre-glass cloth ready for use.

MAKING THE ARMATURE

Begin by assembling the armature – you need to support the outside shape enough that it will not crumple as the weight of the cement coats are added. Every rock form concept is different and a flatter piece will need a lot of horizontal reinforcement but virtually no vertical support, while a standing form like that of the ibigawa rock shown on page 8 and pages 90–91 would require a flat base, an upright shaft and 'T'-form top. Sculptors often use aluminium wire for lightness. Construct a shape strong enough to make a sound basic support for additional external material. Once your armature is set up to the rough shape and size and feels firm, you can move on to the next stage.

BUILDING THE CONTOURS

You now need to fill out the form, which is done by wrapping chicken wire around the armature and securing it to the core with wires. Then comes the enormously satisfying job of crumpling and bending the chicken wire to fashion the desired form. Take time with this and consider it from every angle. You can always attach extra bits to extend the lines, but this is the most convenient time to do it. Make sure all the chicken wire is secured to the armature. When you are satisfied with the shape, you can prepare the fibre-glass cloth.

Cut sufficient strips of fibre-glass cloth to cover every surface of the chicken wire. Fibre-glass cloth is used because it conforms to the shape without springing up or refusing to stay in place like fibre-glass mat.

ADDING CIMENT FONDU

When you are confident you have enough cloth prepared, you can go ahead and make up a sloppy mix of ciment fondu and water. Do not mix more than you can use quickly, say in an hour.

I found that an old kitchen mixing bowl, a spoon and an old coffee mug made for convenient preparation and application. Dip an old paint brush in the cement 'goop' and start dabbing it on

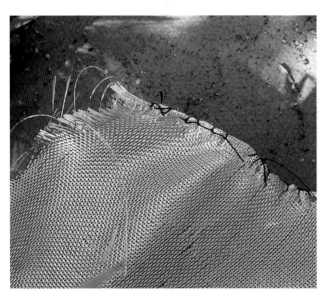

An armature with chicken-wire netting wired on to it.

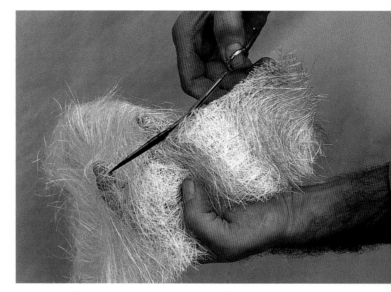

Cutting the fibre-glass cloth into strips for ease of use.

Constructing an armature for a tall rock form.

The reinforcing armature and fibre-glass cloth.

so that it penetrates the fibre-glass cloth. Continue working with mugfuls of goop until one side of the 'rock' is completely plastered. Cover with wet cloths, wrap with polythene and leave to harden. Hardening takes place within about four hours and 'curing' (keeping the cement wet while it sets) in 24 hours. After curing, remove the wrapping and cover the fibre-glass cloth on the other side of the 'rock' with goop, making sure you seal over the edges of the dried concrete half. The second side is then wrapped up and cured as for the first side.

Successive complete coats of ciment fondu are then added and cured until you judge the concrete shell to be thick enough. Colour may be added to different coats to help distinguish 'where you have been' as the layers are built up over each other. You can trowel on thicker mixes of ciment fondu, sand and water when you want to build details like crevices and strata. If this entails adding fresh cement to a dried area, remember to add a layer of goop first to 'key' the new coat to the old. Let your creation dry to a slow cure – this strengthens the concrete and the final result should be strong but hopefully nowhere near as heavy as 'real' rock.

The final touch is to add moss pieces or to seed moss into the last layer of wet cement so that it sticks on firmly. Ciment fondu on its own dries to a pleasant dark grey colour and the growth of moss soon naturalizes the appearance still further.

A completed horizontal slab of rock planted with junipers.

CREATING OTHER FORMS

The horizontal slab arrangement planted with junipers shown in the photograph below is another example of the technique – and how natural this planting looks. Think of the possibilities this presents: how about a series of wooded islands of different sizes displayed on a sea of sand? Or the same on a huge slab of smoked glass? All these images are heroic in size but can be just as interesting if made very small.

It is also possible to make any additional rocks and stones you need from ciment fondu. If you need any hard-to-get rock forms or fancy some matched shapes for your landscapes, this technique is the one for you. Ciment fondu can also be lightened in colour either by adding another cement called Secar

250 (which is white) at the mixing stage, or by rubbing small amounts of the enamel paints modellers use into the grain of the dried cement. A little experimentation will give you some wonderful effects. Remember to use the camouflage technique of adding darker colour to the recesses to enhance the shadows and suggest other forms.

To those who remain sceptical about the durability of cement casting, I would say that as I write this I possess a 'firefly' stone lantern, modelled on the one in the Katsura Imperial Villa, made 33 years ago. Its texture has fooled people ever since it was made and it remains in excellent condition.

Another idea: chicken wire is wrapped around a pot, allowing you to 'pot' the tree in the rock without root disturbance or any worry about the presence of fresh lime.

The chicken wire and fibre-glass cloth together give an appreciation of the final result.

The back view. A base is added to the bottom of the rock structure to support the pot, which is inserted from the back. Wet newspapers are then stuffed into the cavity behind and around the pot, and a layer of moss is added to disguise the pot completely.

The completed image of a tree growing on an island or out of a rocky outcrop is totally convincing.

creating miniature landscapes

Having looked at the various tools, materials and techniques you will need, as well as the plants themselves, it is now time to start on the really exciting bit: creating your own miniature bonsai landscapes. Each project in this section gives details of how to assemble one of the landscapes described in Chapter 1. Use them as the practical starting point for your own experiments and designs, learn about techniques and borrow ideas – and then have fun creating your own unique miniature landscapes.

AFTERCARE

In hot areas or countries, and in mild climates during hot spells, you must shade newly potted and newly styled trees. Even after receiving only minor work, trees need a recuperative period in a shade house. Restyled trees are at risk because their bark can dry out in hot sun where pruning and wiring have created openings in the bark. While a little sun scorch and wind desiccation will only damage the leaves, a lot can cause branches to die back or may even kill the tree.

The notes on aftercare that are included in the projects are specifically for those plants. In general terms, trees need to be shaded, watered carefully and fed according to the individual care schedules given in the Tree Care Directory. Those trees lacking special aftercare notes below received only minor work or are the subject of general discussion where the styling programme was phased over a long period.

chinese juniper

SEVEN-TRUNK RAFT ON IBIGAWA ROCK

(See page 8)

COMPONENTS

Ibigawa rock Height: 60cm (24in). Bonsai nurseries import this from Japan.

Chinese juniper Height: 60cm (24in). Source: garden centres and bonsai nurseries. *Note* If you choose a heavy trunk, you will have trouble bending it to fit the contours of the rock.

Clay+peat+topsoil Pre-mixed to a stiff paste with water. It must 'stay' when applied.

Training wire Thick enough to bend the trunk, probably 5mm aluminium. For detailing the tree, use 1mm, 1.5mm, 2mm and 2.5mm gauges.

Tools and sundries Wire cutters, branch pruners, trimming shears, rake, wound sealant, scalpel and pliers, hormone rooting powder, pressure pads such as foam rubber, soil mix, drainage mesh.

Container Oval. Size: 52.5 x 37.5 x 6.25cm (21 x 15 x 2½in). Colour: grey/brown unglazed. Bonsai nurseries import these from Japan, or you can have one made.

Mosses

METHOD

Assemble this raft in spring.

Consider the rock carefully: it will have a lot of interesting texture. Ibigawa rock comes in a series of deep greys that can include the colours seen on a pigeon's neck: deep green and red to black. Many have white quartz outcropping, as on the one belonging to the Andersons. Choose a rock tall enough to do the job and make sure it is stable. If you see one you like that is a bit wobbly, it may be possible to saw or grind the base so that it sits better – ibigawa rock is often filed and shaped in Japan.

Pre-wire the tree, trunk and branches. You may be wiring to waste if these are pruned off, but it saves time to do it all now and gives you various alternatives.

Select a planting zone that will not hide the best features of the rock. This may sound obvious, but it is easy to make a mistake when you are starting out. Imagine the tree sitting on the rock and how the branches/'trunks' will be placed, and let that help you make your decision. Smear the planting zone with the soil paste – this is great fun! Shade the rock.

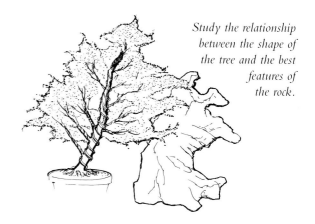

Study the relationship between the shape of the tree and the best features of the rock.

Consider the juniper trunk in relation to the rock. Look for how the two can best be married so that the branches work with the protrusions of the rock. When you are satisfied, remove the branches on the side of the trunk that will attach to the rock. Cut and peel bark windows along the in-facing side of the juniper and dust with hormone rooting powder. Unpot the tree, comb out the roots and 'offer' the tree to the rock.

Study the branches of the tree and protrusions of the rock, then add the paste over the planting zone.

When you are satisfied, bend the tree to the rock shape and twist-wire it on to the paste-smeared planting zone, ensuring that the cut windows are submerged in the paste. Add pressure pads over the trunk where the friction points fall and twist-tighten the wires to bring the trunk firmly on to the rock. Tuck the roots under and around the base of the rock. Shade the rock/tree unit and mist the roots.

Prepare the pot in the usual way with drainage mesh and bottom soil. Stand the rock/tree unit in the container and carefully plant the roots. Add soil, pot up in the usual way and water in well.

 The tree wired to the rock.

Arrange the pre-wired branches/'trunks'. Spend time on this and try to take advantage of the shape of the rock to make the branch/trunk lines flow out naturally from it. Any bushier branches can be divided into lateral pads and will soon help to generate a mature image, even at this early stage.

Thin and prune the foliage to neaten profiles and clean out the underlines. Add more paste so that it laps around the trunk, then place mosses on to it and make sure they key into it, pressing down the edges. Add extra soil to top off the area around the rock, level it and water in once more. If you wish, add a layer of fine sand over the soil to suggest water. Finally, shade the planting and mist the foliage.

AFTERCARE

In areas where there is strong sunlight and high temperatures, or even during a hot spell in a mild climate, dappled shade is the best location for growing potted junipers. Shade is also an absolute must for optimum recovery after restyling and a suitable shade area is easily set up. In the UK, for example, I set up a light wooden cage over my growing bench and used green plastic shade netting that created at least 40 per cent shade.

Once shade has been provided, the condition of a juniper previously grown in full sun will change quite dramatically. All plants have a range of pigment in their leaves which responds to light: those in sun tend to be yellow and those in shade to be dark blue-green. Traditionally, it is claimed that bonsai do best in full sun with a meagre water supply, but this is only partly true. What is actually meant by that dangerously over-simplified statement is that sunlight provides ultraviolet light which induces a dwarfer type of top growth, and that moderate watering holds back excess growth. Unfortunately, this advice is all too often followed so slavishly that it leads first to drought, then to yellow/brown leaf scorching and miserably hard and thin new growth, and in extreme cases to die-back of the branches.

Moderately shaded junipers are full of moisture, their foliage is full and soft, there is copious budding and the colour deepens to a healthy green. In fact, you will see an almost bluish bloom of health on the leaves. Do not use dense shade, but make sure there is enough to give significant relief from the sun – the effect should be like walking round the side of a house into the 'bright' shade. I once visited a nursery in California on a day when the wind brought scorching heat straight from the Mojave desert. The stock consisted mostly of azaleas and they looked dry and yellow in the sun. Inside a wood-lathe growing house, however, conditions were totally different. The roof was made from shade cloth and the ground was covered with damp redwood bark – and there were lush, strong shoots on all the wonderfully green trees.

Feeding

Nitrogen is invaluable in promoting sound green growth. I prefer to use a water-soluble feed: something like Miracle-Gro is very good and makes for deep foliage colour and strong growth. If you do give a granular slow-release feed, make sure you under-do the dose.

Watering

Keep junipers damp, and in hot weather mist the leaves frequently.

trident maple

FIVE-TRUNK CLUMP STYLE
(See page 10)

COMPONENTS

Five trident maple seedlings or cuttings Height:
30–60cm (12–24in). Source: bonsai nurseries; some
specialist tree nurseries carry trident maples for landscape work. Search in the growing season so that you
can check leaf characteristics, and select specimens with
uniform leaf size, shape and colour. Leaves with
straightish edges without conspicuous teeth and a blue
underside seem to colour especially brilliantly in
autumn. The growing-season leaf colour of this strain is
a dark green and new shoots are very red.

Training wire Thick enough to bend the trunks, probably
4mm aluminium. For detailing the trees, use 1mm,
1.5mm, 2mm and 2.5mm gauges.

Tools and sundries Wire cutters, branch pruners, trimming shears, rake, wound sealant, plastic tape, soil mix,
plant location grid, drainage mesh.

Container Oval. Size: 25 x 20 x 7.5cm (10 x 8 x 3in).
Colour: mottled yellow glaze.

Mosses

METHOD

Begin work on this clump in spring, just as the buds swell.

Select five trunks that will work well together. Look for
different heights, curvy trunks that are similar in feeling
and varying trunk thicknesses. Check for surface roots or
any that look and feel as if they could be. Take time over
the selection – you can often find great things to utilize in
making clump arrangements, such as trunks with multiple
base shoots. When you are happy with the selection, try
one last test: if the trunk does not have any curves or movement, can you bend it a little? If not, leave it where it is!

If you have exhausted your sources and still not found
an ideal combination, do not give up – just buy those clos-
est to the ideal and take them home and develop them a
little. Plant the trees in a box with plenty of root-run and
let them grow on freely; they will soon fatten up. When you
plant them for the first time, take care to spread the roots
radially around the trunk: this takes only a couple of
moments, and the gain in decorative value when a tree has
buttressed roots is well worth it.

If the problem is lack of curvature, cut the trunks back
hard and leave them to re-sprout and grow away strongly.
You can easily control the shape of the new growth with
gentle wiring. If you want to separate the trunks in terms of
size and thickness, you might consider using pots of different sizes, matching the tallest trunk to the biggest pot and
so on. Let those which are going to be major lines develop
and carry a lot of leaves, and scale down the loading for the
smaller trunks. This works because the wood fattens according to the work it is called on to do. Feed the maples freely
from a month after they have been planted, using Miracid at
half strength every week – and watch those maples grow!
Towards late summer, switch the feed to 0–10–10, given
every month. Trim the trees back lightly in the autumn.

In the second year the maples may be wired, but keep a
careful lookout for wires biting into wood – trident maples
grow and thicken fast. Continue to feed as in the first
season. De-wire the trees by autumn at the latest.

The trees are assembled in the third spring as the buds
begin to swell. Unpot the trees and comb out and wash off

the roots. Eliminate any dominant lower roots and any that are darkened: the aim is to encourage young and vigorous feeder roots. Prepare the location grid at this stage. Make sure it is the right size to fit inside the temporary growing container and then thread location wires through the grid mesh. Add drainage mesh and bottom soil to the container.

Look at each root system carefully and prepare it by pruning back about one-third of the overall mass. The tallest tree is usually placed first, then the secondary tree and so on. Placement is really a matter of taste, but in the case of the Andersons' group, smaller trunks were placed in the foreground, and when trained to curve outwards this placement is rather attractive. Just avoid too many conflicting lines and angles. Adjacency (the relative proximity of the grouped trunks, as shown in the tree placement diagram on page 95) is a useful tool when planning the trunk arrangement. Trident maples can accept quite radical root reduction provided the top growth is also thinned out to preserve the balance of moisture. Such trees also need shaded aftercare to compensate for their reduced root system, until the roots can 'kick in' and grow vigorously once more.

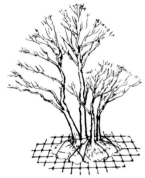

Left: *Assembling the clump.*
Below: *Bonding the trunks.*

When you are confident that the trees work together, and to achieve the look of fusion seen in the Andersons' group, a secondary tree may be bonded to the main one by slicing the rootball to allow close placement, and further by removing bark flaps on the converging trunks so that they may be induced to graft together. Place the peeled areas together and bind them in place with plastic tape. Paint the area with wound sealant to exclude the air and to keep the union moist. The graft should be complete within a year and the bonded trunks will give an instant aged look to the planting. Twist-tie the root systems of the trees to the grid, place the grid in the container and tie it in place. Add soil, taking care that it penetrates every part of the roots. Spend time spreading the surface roots, then cover them. Place clumps of fine moss between the main roots, making sure

that it is bedded in well. Water in well and shade the clump.

Branches are best shortened a little at this stage to give the roots a chance to really get going. After a month or so, when the clump has settled in, you can resume feeding and shaping the trees. Allow the new growth to make two to three pairs of leaves, then wire it and allow it to grow freely until the wires tighten. Remove the wires and cut back the branches. Allow the shoots to make two to three pairs of leaves and then cut them back. Trim the branches back hard in the autumn to keep growth building slowly.

The roots of trident maples thicken nicely and web together to make a woody structure of fused roots that flows out from the clump of trunks. Keep them covered as long as you can bear to, as moist roots thicken faster than those which are exposed too soon. When you brush away the soil and uncover the roots, they begin to form thicker bark, which will soon match the trunk texture.

AFTERCARE

In hot areas and countries, and in mild climates during hot spells, you must shade potted trident maples. This tree has received minor work but it still needs recuperation in a shade house.

Use the shaded conditions described for the junipers in Project 1 – I remember seeing fully grown Japanes maples inside shade houses in Holland, where there was otherwise no wind protection from the North Sea gales, and the trees were just fine. The leaf colour of shade-protected trident maples is deep green, with some reddening, and the new shoots are deep red and vigorous.

Feeding

Feed with Miracid at half strength, twice a month from immediately after restyling through until midsummer to keep the tree green and happy. Give 0-10-10 once a month from late summer to early autumn to harden off the growth. From late summer, let the sun reach the maples for a couple of hours or so each day and you will get autumn colour.

Watering

After restyling, be careful to keep the tree damp. Drought at this time may weaken pruned branch zones, allowing them to dry up. Evening leaf misting is beneficial. Remember to seal all pruning cuts with one of the suggested wound preparations to maintain the wood in a turgid state – dry wood does not bud.

chinese elm

SEVEN-TRUNK LANDSCAPE (SAIKEI)

(See page 12)

COMPONENTS

Five short Chinese elms Actual bonsai, or cuttings or seedlings. Height: 12.5–25cm (5–10in). Source: bonsai nurseries carry imported Chinese elms of various types and batches of propagations. Search in the growing season so that you can check leaf characteristics: select those with uniform leaf size and colour. There is a lot of variation among elms and batches do get mixed up. Look for nice bark and dark green, healthy leaves. In Tim's group, trunk diameters range from single- to two-finger thickness. Make sure to get these, as they give the necessary depth to the planting.

Training wire Thick enough to bend the trunks if required, probably 4mm aluminium. For detailing the trees, use 1mm, 1.5mm, 2mm and 2.5mm gauges.

Tools and sundries Wire cutters, branch pruners, trimming shears, rake, wound sealant, soil mix, plant location grid, drainage mesh.

Container Rectangular. Size: 60 x 37.5 x 7.5cm (24 x 15 x 3in). Colour: blue/green glaze. Bonsai nurseries import these from Japan. Actually, I think this pot is too deep for this group, and the glaze is a bit 'mechanical'. Try to find a potter whose containers are better made and who has some understanding of the subtleties of glazing. If you are stuck with imported pots, a shallower pot in an unglazed light grey would work. Beware the rash of cheap-quality Korean and Chinese ceramics that are flooding the market: they are a bit too heavy-looking for this project.

Stones About 12–15 matching stones, grey to silvery in colour with horizontal strata. You could make these yourself using the ciment fondu method (see Chapter 6) – it is an interesting process and gives you total control.

Sand Fine grey sand for finishing the 'lake' surface.

Mosses Try to locate sheets of moss if possible. Choose a low-growing variety.

METHOD

Assemble this landscape in spring, just as the buds swell.

Unpot the elms and check the condition of the roots. If they are very root-bound there may well be some heavy lower roots that must be removed. Pre-wire the elms, as this is kinder to the trees than doing it after they have been root-pruned. Comb out the roots, prune and balance the mass so that there are no 'heroes' left to dominate among the lower roots, reducing the total mass by about one-third. Keep the roots damp. (Any heavy lower roots that have been removed can be potted up as cuttings and will sprout as trees in their own right – a lot of imported elms begin life as root divisions of this kind.)

Check that the location grid really fits the container and is the same size as the planting area, trimming it down if required. Pass location wires through the mesh

Location grid fitted to the container.

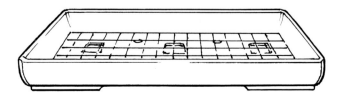

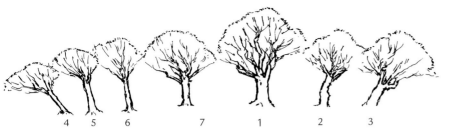

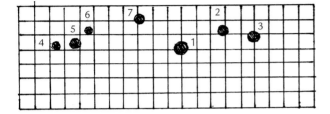

Tree placement.

and prepare the pot with drainage mesh, location tie wires and bottom soil (see page 67).

Take the grid and site the major tree (1); in this case, place it to the right of centre of the long axis and a little behind the centre of the minor axis. Twist-tie it loosely in position. Add the two other fairly thick trunks (2, 3) to the right and further back, so that they are halfway between the main tree and the back edge of the pot, and twist-tie them loosely. Check their relative positions and adjust for preferred trunk lines, angles and posture. Make sure the ground plan of the trunk placement creates an interesting pattern and avoid a straight line. Aim for a triangular planting pattern.

Locate the three lesser trunks (4, 5, 6) as another triangle, placing it well to the left. Rotate and check their placement for the best trunk line and angle, then twist-tie them loosely. Make sure the space between the outer trunk and the pot rim is smaller than the space at the right-hand edge of the planting. You will find this asymmetrical placement is pleasing to the eye – dumping it centrally is boring. The placement along the minor axis is also interesting, and either forward of the right-hand triangle or to the rear of it will work.

The seventh tree is placed slightly to the right of centre between the two trunk groups and splits the distance at the back between the rear-most trunk and the pot rim. Check the placement and angle, then twist-tie loosely into position. Lift the grid and the attached group and try it in the pot. Adjust the placement again if necessary. When you are satisfied, lift the grid out again, build the soil level as required, replace the grid and twist-tie it firmly. The final touch is to lift and feature the surface roots. When you have done this, cover them again and twist-tie the trees just firmly enough for them not to topple. Add more soil and make sure it penetrates the roots adequately. Bend and shape the pre-wired trees so that the trunk and branch lines all harmonize. Seal any cuts of more than matchstick thickness.

Place the stones to make an interesting irregular line, to give visual credence and physical support for the banking of the soil. Set the stones in a little, so that they seem to rise naturally from the soil. Mound the soil into two shallow hills, bringing it up to and behind the line of stones forming the edge. Water the planting well with a fine spray until the surplus drips from the holes. Soak the sheet moss and press it on to the mounded soil, making sure the edges sit down properly. Water again and shade the group. Finally, spread the fine sand in front of the stone river/lake bank to simulate water and level it off.

AFTERCARE

In general, elms can take a lot of sun. I have seen them grown extensively in full sun in Spain where temperatures are really cooking and they seem just fine – as long as they are watered! When it becomes desirable to protect an elm, say after a major repotting session or following a lot of pruning, be careful not to leave the tree in deep shade for too long, as prolonged light deprivation will kill twigs and even branches. Overwintering in too dark a place, for example, can cost you half a tree – I remember keeping one totally frost free only to have it do that, so you soon learn!

Feeding
Avoid too much nitrogen – it fattens every part of the tree (see feeding recommendations for Project 4).

Watering
Never allow an elm to dry out as it will sulk and refuse to bud where you want it to, even to the extent of shedding the branch you have just spent five years building up – only to bud again from its base.

'seiju' elm

NINE-TREE GROUP
(See page 14)

COMPONENTS

Nine or more 'Seiju' elms Bonsai or, more likely, propagations. Height: 25–60cm (10–24in). Source: Bonsai nurseries. Select plants with deep green leaves. Avoid any with conspicuous die-back, as these are often riddled with scale insects or have been. Choose trunk diameters from single- to two-finger thickness. Look for pleasing trunk lines: they do not have to be rigidly upright. Look also for trees with an attractive head of branches that have been pinched back for density and taper. Heavy upper branch lines can be diffi-cult to handle, as they tend to fatten the top of the tree and spoil the winter silhouette – so walk by those too.

Training wire Thick enough to bend the trunks if required. This species is brittle and my way of handling this problem is to use over-kill with the wire gauge and to wire loosely: the factors of extra strength and gentle but firm contact make for sure and easy leverage when the wood is bent (like a giant man picking up a two-year-old child, the excess energy makes the process safer). Therefore, 5mm aluminium wire would probably be good. For detailing the trees, use 1mm, 1.5mm, 2mm and 2.5mm gauges.

Tools and sundries Wire cutters, branch pruners, trim-ming shears, rake, wound sealant, soil mix, plant location grid, drainage mesh.

Container Oval. Size: 60 x 45 x 6.25cm (24 x 18 x 2½in). Colour: grey/brown, made from a mica compound. A cheap, acceptable solution for establishing the planting, and a much better option than an inappropriate ceramic pot.

Mosses

METHOD

Assemble this group in spring, just as the buds swell.

Follow the instructions on root pruning, pre-wiring and sizing of the location grid given in Project 3.

Check the trunks and branches for any substantial pruning scars: the wood will be extra-hard at these points and will need special attention. Bend the pre-wired trees as necessary. Use your hands overlapped together and squeeze and bend simultaneously – trunk lines are corrected easily by this technique. If any trunk or branch seems especially unwilling, add another strand of wire and try again. If you support the wood as described you will not break it. The reason for shaping prior to planting is to get round the problem of blundering through brittle growth as you attempt to make major adjustments. That is when branches get broken.

Site the major tree on the location grid. This time it is placed to the left of centre along the major axis and forward of centre on the minor axis. Twist-tie it loosely in position. The Andersons' main tree has a pair of subsidiary trunks attached to it (1+2+3). One is from a very low bud on the trunk and the other grows directly from the strong surface root line to the left. Place the secondary trunk (4)

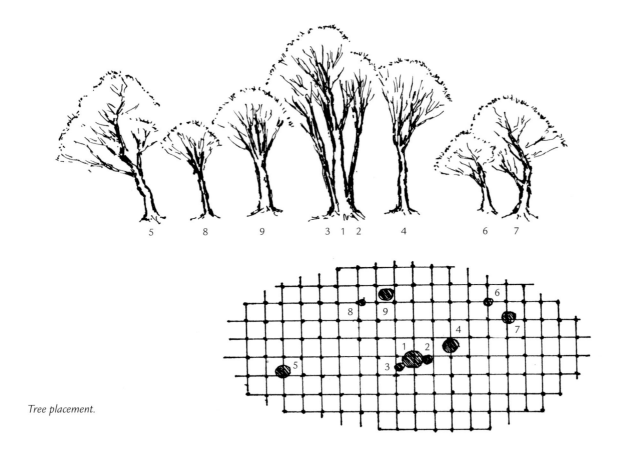

Tree placement.

to the right of the main tree and further back, and twist-tie it in place. The large tree at the left (5) of the group goes in next. It is positioned fairly close to the edge of the pot and slightly in advance of the main tree. Avoid jamming it right against the edge or letting it appear to, as visually this is uncomfortable. The original tree looks a shade too close.

Now place the two right-hand trees next (6, 7) well back from the major centre line. Finally, add the last two trees (8, 9), placing them right at the back and to the left of the major tree so that they appear to add to its weight. They also add depth and richness to the grove, so are pretty important!

Check the trunk placement for diversity of the ground pattern and make fine adjustments if necessary for better trunk lines, angles and the variety of negative spaces they create. Then complete the planting, twist-tying the trees to firm them on the grid.

Add more soil, making sure it is fully in contact with all the intermeshing root masses. Adjust the shapes so that all the trees work together and seal any pruning cuts. Spread the surface roots and cover them. Mound the soil and water everything in well. Place the moss and water in again. Shade the planting.

AFTERCARE

Follow the recommendations for the Chinese elms in Project 3. Any major pruning is best done using a two-step system. Leave an initial, generous length of stub that can dry up naturally and will not affect adjacent live tissue. This is pruned close later, at the end of the season. In this way, the wound heals flat without the big, fat healing callus that develops in the active growing season. On a delicate-looking tree like this, these callus swellings can be a visual disaster.

Feeding

Regular feeding is the key to a satisfactory design programme. Never give too much nitrogen to an elm, as it will thicken up and coarsen. Use a couple of shots of half-strength Miracle-Gro as the trees leaf out in the spring. After that change to Fish Emulsion, and your trees will stay green and will not fatten too fast.

western hemlock

FIVE-TRUNK GROUP ON ROCK
(See page 16)

COMPONENTS

Five small Western hemlocks Height: 15–35cm (6–14in).
Source: collect from the wild or purchase from nurseries.
Look for trunks with some character and different thicknesses, and for compact, dense branches. If you want to
use a dwarf cultivar, there is a lot to be said for choosing
one of the many varieties of the Eastern hemlock, *Tsuga
canadensis*. Transplant the trees in spring and use smallish
square plastic pots. Grow the trees for a year so that they
are established before they are styled.

Training wire Thick enough to bend the trunks, probably
3mm aluminium. For detailing the trees, use 1mm,
1.5mm, 2mm and 2.5mm gauges.

Tools and sundries Wire cutters, branch pruners, trimming
shears, rake, wound sealant, soil mix, plant location grid
(optional), drainage mesh.

Rock Size: 75 x 22.5 x 15cm (30 x 9 x 6in). Unless you are
extraordinarily lucky and find a stunning rock like the one
shown above, by far the best option is to reproduce it using
the ciment fondu technique (see Chapter 6).

Mosses

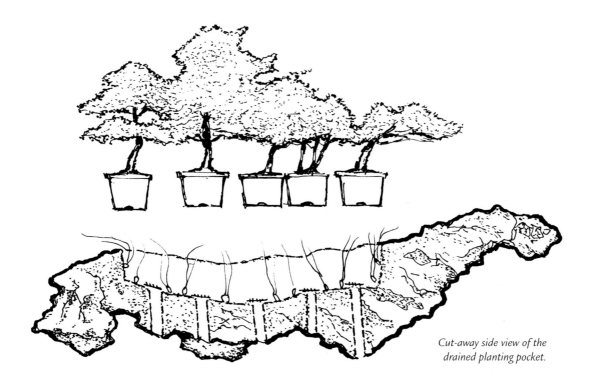

*Cut-away side view of the
drained planting pocket.*

METHOD

Assemble this group in spring.

When building your rock using the ciment fondu technique, incorporate a cavity accessible from the back of the rock that is big enough to accept the root systems of the trees, pot and all (see page 87). Alternatively, make it a drained planting pocket that accepts the potted plants from the top, in which case there is no need to stuff the back with paper and moss to mask the pots – they are simply dropped into place and disappear, surrounded by soil and moss.

The diagram shows the tie wires which are added to locate the pots snugly in the planting cavity. This clever system frees you up to create the rock just as you want it, even allowing you to customize it to suit some special tree or planting arrangement.

Pre-wire and style the trees, going for a low contour that will hug the rock. Move the pots to simulate group placement: the square pots will fit neatly together. Style each tree so that it contributes to the overview of general contours, branch planes and allied trunk forms.

Prepare the planting cavity in the rock by adding a layer of soil and bed the pots into it one by one, building the group as you go. Tie the pots in and make fine adjustments to the branch planes and contours once more. Seal any pruning cuts. Add soil over the pots to mask their edges and water in well. Add moss and water again lightly. Shade the planting.

AFTERCARE

Potted hemlocks grow best if kept permanently in light shade. Other styles would look wonderful if planted in this way. Suppose, for example, you fancied a multi-trunked image that was developed from a raft or a root-connected style. You could further refine the design by styling it as a leaning or windswept image.

The great thing with designing your tree and rock form together is that you can create marvellous harmonies of sympathetic lines that really blend these elements together. Such arrangements delight the eye and you can add details like small flowering azaleas or quinces for colour accents. Try using differently coloured mosses as well.

'kingsville' box

11-TREE LANDSCAPE
(See page 18)

COMPONENTS

11 'Kingsville' box Height: 7.5–25cm (3–10in). Source: bonsai nurseries and the better garden centres. 'Kingsville' box is now more easily come by than when the Enwrights assembled their landscape, but it remains a desirable and unusual plant both in the garden and as a miniature land-scape species.Look for different trunk thickness and multiple formation.

Training wire Thick enough to bend the trunks if required, probably 2mm aluminium. Use it in the upper trunk, which is thinner – older and thicker wood is very brittle. For detailing the trees, use 1mm, 1.5mm and 2mm gauges.

Tools and sundries Wire cutters, branch pruners, trim-ming shears, rake, wound sealant, soil mix, plant location grid (optional), drainage mesh.

Container Oval. Size: 45 x 35 x 5cm (18 x 14 x 2in). Colour: brown unglazed.

Stones A selection of quite rugged small and medium-sized stones in greys and browns. Select stones with an overall similarity of shape, as this helps to unify the design.

Sand Small shingle and medium-grade gravel. Try to find sand with a greyish colour rather than the bright tone of crushed flint.

Mosses Look for flat sheet moss and include some with a different colour and texture.

METHOD

Assemble this group in spring.

Pre-wire and style the trees, and arrange them roughly in the ground pattern you see in the photograph of the Enwrights' group. Here the planting zone is crescent-shaped, with its points swinging towards the viewer. Its depth from the back edge of the pot to the bank edged with stones is about 17.5cm (7in).

It will help a lot if you stand your plants on blocks of wood or heaps of soil mix to simulate the different heights in the planting. You can then adjust the contours again so that they work better as an overall unit. You will notice that in these projects we keep coming back to the unity factor: it is worth its weight in gold as a design concept and is common to all art forms. Absorb this principle and use it. Good questions to ask yourself as you design and style away are: 'Do the lines work together? If not, why not?'

Prepare the pot with drainage mesh, and if you think you will work better with it, make a customized plant loca-tion grid. If you make the grid from wire, it will be infi-nitely bendable and can rise and fall with the mounded soil. Pass location wires through the drainage holes of the container and through the grid if you are using it. Add a layer of bottom soil to the container, then mound it to form the crescent-shaped planting zone towards the back of the pot. Do not add too much at this stage – just enough to seat the plants initially is enough if you are planting directly into the container. Direct planting means less root disturbance for the plant.

If you are using the grid, mound the soil up more because the grid sits on it and curves with the mound. Grid planting means more root disturbance as the roots must be spread to sit on it, but they quickly root through into the soil and you may prefer to use it for the stability it offers the trunks as you assemble everything. It is an easy matter to shape the grid to the mound – just bend it and check it in place until it fits.

If you are planting directly into the mound, begin by unpotting the trees and combing out about one-third of the outer roots to give you some lateral lines; keep the roots damp. Place the main tree (1) first, slightly right of

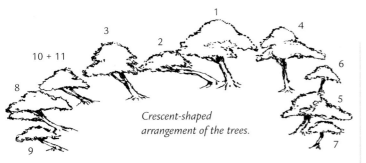

Crescent-shaped arrangement of the trees.

the centre along the major axis line. It needs to be forward on the mound. Place the secondary trunk (2) behind the main tree and to the right, with a left tilt so that it passes behind the main tree. Place the third tree (3) to the left of the main one and close to it with a tilt to the left. Check the position, front view and planting angle, adjust and then add more soil, making sure it penetrates the roots.

Place the tallest top right-hand tree on the mound (4), then the nearest big tree in the right foreground below it on the tip of the crescent (5). Make sure that the main negative area above the foreground tree and below the background tree stays clearly defined: those are the key trees on the right-hand side of the planting. Fit the other two minor trunks (6, 7) to the right of these so that their lines round out and extend the main contours. When you are happy with their positions, add more soil as before.

Next move to the left foreground. Place the larger tree on the left (8). Make sure its crown is on a line that falls halfway up that main negative area on the right. You have now completed the difficult bit! Add the little left foreground tree (9), making sure you place it on a different line to the trees in the right foreground – you must keep that asymmetry going. When you are happy with everything, add more soil and firm the plants a little.

The last to go in are the two trunk lines (10, 11) up on the hill that interrupt the space between the main tree and the large tree on the left. Place them at about one-third of that distance from the left. These minor lines are important to the flow of the design and need to curve and tilt to the left. Place and check them, and when you are happy with how they look, add more soil and firm in. Stand back and check everything – literally put distance between you and the design. Artists know the value of doing this – it simplifies the image, focusing attention on both the good and bad points. Fine-tune your image as seems indicated. Often you will find that smoothing the contours with detailed grooming will be all you need to do – at this stage!

Set the stones in so that they bed into the soil naturally. Add more soil in the foreground to bring it up to the pot rim and level it off. As you work with the stones, from a bird's-eye view you are making a blunted 'V' shape, so let the contours of the stones wander across the levelled soil area. Place them so that they make a random line that goes backwards and forwards. You will see that the stones make a zigzag line from the left that ends almost below the main tree and that the right-hand line comes forward from that point. This creates an illusion of the river springing up from behind those rocks. Place the foreground stones so that they complement the foreground trees but do not make them too big.

Stones set in naturally.

Contour all the soil, eventually bringing it down and behind the stones. Think of how a river bank comes together and sculpt the mounds so that they blend with the lines of the stones. Then water well with a fine spray, making sure the soil is moist. Saturate the moss and place it on the mounded soil. Press all the edges in and pay special attention to the areas around the trees so as not to cover any surface roots. Make sure the stones are well mossed in. You will now begin to appreciate how all this works, and every touch improves the planting.

Finally, pour on a little of the medium-grade grey gravel, taking it right up to lap the stones. Then add some small shingle on top, making it form a stream from where the river appears behind the stones. It will give you 'water' movement – if you do it well enough!

If you are using a planting grid, the whole placement is much the same but you will be more concerned with mounding the soil so that the grid and roots are well buried. The spread roots should be planted deep enough so that they do not pop up if there is any erosion of the soil before everything settles.

AFTERCARE

The trees must be adequately shaded – no amount of soil watering is as effective as the use of dappled shade. 'Kingsville' box are too often seen yellowed by inappropriate sun exposure. They are naturally slow growing, but such treatment slows them to the point where only leaf extension takes place and lateral growth is negligible.

PROJECT 7

japanese maple

11-TRUNK LANDSCAPE/GROUP

(See page 20)

COMPONENTS

11 Japanese maples Height: 20–30cm (8–12in). You will
need to select plants with small leaves and a neat growth
habit. Look for identical leaf and growth characteristics.
Like the Enwrights, you can always take cuttings and so
ensure they will be uniform. I imported a batch of maples
and propagated from them, and kept the same clone
going for over 20 years. A lot of those plants have
become fine trees now, with the same small leaves and
bright autumn colour that first attracted me – it is a
rewarding thing to do. Choose different trunk thicknesses
and look for radial surface roots if possible.

Clay+peat+topsoil Pre-mixed to a stiff paste with water.
It must 'stay' when applied.

Training wire Thick enough to bend the trunks, probably
2mm aluminium. For detailing the trees, use 1mm and
1.5mm gauges.

Tools and sundries Wire cutters, branch pruners, trimming shears, rake, wire mesh for supporting the roots on
the rock, wound sealant, soil mix, drainage mesh.

Rock Size: 37.5 x 10 x 15cm (15 x 4 x 6in). Colour:
grey/brown. Texture rough and scooped out here and
there.

Container Oval. Size: 50 x 37.5 x 5cm (20 x 15 x 2in).
Colour: brown unglazed.

Mosses

METHOD

Begin work on this group in spring, just as the buds swell.

First prepare the maples by pre-wiring, shaping and
pruning. If they need development for trunk thickness,
follow the suggestions for developing trident maples in
Project 2.

The rock is in the form of a weathered turtle-back and
contributes the rising curve to the line of trees planted
along it. This type of design looks strong and borrows
from the visual power of the rock. The way in which the
trees are planted serves to strengthen the links with the
rock, as the roots are developed in a narrow band of soil
and have nowhere to go but to run laterally along the crest
of the rock. They soon thicken and give the wonderful base
you see in the Enwrights' planting, where all the trees seem
to flow from one another.

Begin by considering the rock faces carefully: you will
be covering the back, so be sure to expose the more attractive one! When you are happy with your selection, smear
the pre-mixed soil paste thickly over the back face of the
rock. Cut double lengths of tie wire long enough to pass
up and over the rock and be twist-tied on to it. Stand the
rock on the pairs of wires so that they protrude to the
front and back, ready to be drawn up, first to hold the tree
and then to support its root mass as each one is wrapped
in mesh as the planting proceeds.

Tie-wires ready to be drawn up over the rock to hold the trees.

Arrangement of the trees.

Unpot the trees and comb out the roots, removing any heavy lower ones. Spread the roots, taking care to place the surface ones radially.

Take the tallest and biggest tree (1) and place it to the left, just over the crest of the rock at the back. Twist-tie it and spread the roots sideways and down the back of the rock, pressing them gently into the paste. Add the other trunks to the right of the main one. There are two major trees (2, 3) and two minor ones (4, 5) in this first group. Secure them and spread their roots. Both major trees are significantly shorter than the main tree. Take time with the lateral positioning of the trees, as the negative spaces are subtle: the two major trees are placed so that the right-hand one is one-quarter of the way along the rock from the right. The second tree is placed halfway between the right-hand tree and the main one, and the minor lines divide the space between the second tree and the right-hand one.

Now place two trees at the right-hand end almost above the end of the rock (6, 7). The trunks should be placed closely and echo each other in form. The right-hand end tree extends the foliage canopy some way out. The height of these two trees is halfway between the main tree and the previous two. When the position is correct, twist-tie and secure them.

The two left-hand trees (8, 9) are placed now, right at the end of the rock at the left. The trunks are placed close together, with the minor one at the edge and the heavier one so that it swings right towards the line of the main tree. Twist-tie them and secure the roots.

The last two trees (10, 11) are placed close together halfway up the rock on the left. The height of their peripheries should almost reach that of the main tree. Twist-tie them and secure the roots.

Now distance yourself from the group and consider the effect. When you are happy, add a lot more paste over the roots and make sure it penetrates all round them. Pass a strip of wire mesh horizontally over the adjacent roots, cut wide enough to support the vertical root mass against the rock face. Bring the reserve wires up and twist-tie across the rootballs so that everything is supported. Then tighten the wires enough to hold the planting firmly but without root constriction. Add another layer of paste over the mesh to disguise it. Plant saturated moss on the paste.

Prepare the container with drainage mesh and bottom soil. Carefully place the rock/tree unit and wiggle it into the soil so that it beds in well. Place it just to the rear of the major axis line. Add more soil, mounding it over the lower edges of the draped-down roots. These will then grow on down to the pot soil and develop quickly. Add extra contrast mosses if you wish. Small ferns or dwarf mondo grass would also work next to the massive rock.

Adjust the trunk lines and branches a little so that everything blends in and seal all cuts. Then water well and shade the planting.

The trees securely twist-tied to the rock.

PROJECT 8

european hornbeam

MULTI-TRUNK GROUP

(See page 22)

COMPONENTS

Hornbeams Height: 15–67.5cm (6–27in). Source: seen together, a number of wild collected hornbeams often have trunk forms that appear to blend together, suggesting a combination like this group. They offer the advantages of aged appearance and mature bark and it is worth looking for them. Failing that, European hornbeams are often sold as hedging material. Cuttings are a reliable way to go, too, if you find a plant whose characteristics you particularly like. I have found several with nicely compact leaves and an attractive habit of growth and have propagated them with pretty good success. Bonsai nurseries are another source but they are an expensive option. Look for varying trunk thicknesses, surface roots and usable branches that are not too thick to bend.

Training wire Thick enough to bend the trunks, probably 2–3mm aluminium. For detailing the trees, use 1mm and 1.5mm gauges.

Tools and sundries Wire cutters, branch pruners, trimming shears, rake, wound sealant, soil mix, plant location grid, drainage mesh.

Container Oval. Size: 55 x 40 x 5cm (22 x 16 x 2in). Colour: brown unglazed.

Mosses

METHOD

Assemble this group in spring, just as the buds swell.

Begin with root-established trees, whatever the source. If the trunks need development, follow the suggestions given in Project 2. Hornbeams carry an inbuilt bonus for the would-be tree developer and trunk fattener: they respond tremendously well to nitrogen. I once purchased a piece of hedging material and planted it in a large box, sliced the top out, placed it in a polytunnel (hoop-house) and fed and watered it copiously all year. The first thing I remember noticing was how it erupted buds everywhere. These grew into strong shoots, enabling me to wire, grow, prune and develop branches inside a year. The well-spread roots pulled the base of the trunk out as they took off sideways and the whole tree filled out. In fact, it went from little-finger to thumb thickness in a year, with an almost completed branch system. I potted up the tree the following spring and spread the now strongly formed surface roots. A friend insisted on buying it, thinking it was an old collected tree. When I explained, he wanted it even more! Hornbeams can develop quickly with the right techniques.

Prepare the container with drainage mesh and pass location wires through the drainage holes. Add bottom soil. Prepare the plant location grid and pass location wires through the mesh.

Unpot the trees and comb out and prune the roots. Be prepared for this to take some time: hornbeams can generate very dense roots indeed! The wood is also very hard – in Europe it was known as the engineers' wood and was often used for gear teeth – and sometimes you may have to take a fine-toothed saw to the root pad to remove the outer part before you can comb out the inside roots. Keep the roots damp.

Pre-wire and shape the trunks and branches, and beginning with the tallest tree, place and twist-tie them loosely into place. The ground pattern of planting from overhead looks like a series of soft 'S' forms that wind and meander backwards and forwards across the soil surface and create

Arrangement of the trees.   18 17 16 15 14 13 12 11 10 9 8 7 6 5 4 3 2 1 19 20 21 22 23 24 25 etc

a completely natural mood. The thicks and thins show up well and it is possible to see how the artist has used the heavier lines to create telling impact against the daintier ones (see the diagram on the right). It makes a pretty ground pattern and gives nice vistas through the trunk lines. Add more trees, spreading the surface roots as you go.

The original group was placed in a natural and random fashion with a rather pleasing outswing of trunk lines radiating from a point somewhere near the centre. The major tree (1) and at least three others (2, 3, 4) form the highest point, with the next highest group to its immediate left. Moving left, the next group is lower (5, 6, 7), and if my suggestion for rounding out the edges is followed, the left-hand edge can be extended using shorter trunks with left-pointing branches (8–18).

On the right of the tallest group, the next highest point is composed of three trunks (19, 20, 21). The line then steps down and could be rounded and extended outwards, adding minor trunks to the right-hand edge (21–25 and so on). Finally, check the back of the planting for negative spacing that can be made more interesting by sliding some small trunks in there. These give depth and richness to the perspective.

Have fun with all this and enjoy angling and shifting the trunk lines around. The grid is quite wonderful in the flexibility it allows for fine placement. When you are happy with everything, firm up the tie wires so that the trees will not topple. Add more soil and make sure it penetrates through the complex layers of intermeshed roots. Finish by mounding the soil gently and naturally.

Now step back and look critically at your creation.

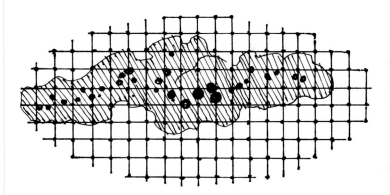

Tree placement.

Detail the trees one by one, bending, shaping and grooming them to smooth off the contours as well as you can. These will get closer and twiggier as the trees grow and are pinched back. Saturate the planting with water and add the mosses, leaving the main root lines exposed. Then water everything in and shade the trees.

AFTERCARE

Feeding

Once the planting is assembled the amount of nitrogen fed to the tree should be minimal, otherwise everything carries on fattening and all branch taper is lost. Give Miracle-Gro at half strength once a month, beginning a month after assembly, until early summer. Give 0-10-10 once a month from midsummer to early autumn. Repeat

american larch

11-TRUNK GROUP
(See page 24)

COMPONENTS

11 American larches Height: 20–65cm (8–26in). Source: collect wild larches if possible, for their trunk character and mature bark. Failing that, larches are available from bonsai and forestry nurseries. Try the forestry nurseries first – you will get a better range of sizes and prices. Check each plant for surface roots: mass-production planting techniques often make for knotted-up roots, so avoid trees with these malformed bases as the roots on older larches are difficult to realign. It is better to buy smaller trees and correct the root formation to your satisfaction.

Training wire Thick enough to bend the trunks, probably 2.5–3mm aluminium. For detailing the trees, use 1mm, 1.5mm and 2mm gauges.

Tools and sundries Wire cutters, branch pruners, trimming shears, rake, wound sealant, soil mix, plant location grid, drainage mesh.

Container Rectangular. Size: 45 x 35 x 5cm (18 x 14 x 2in). Colour: muted yellow, grey or blue glaze. Unglazed light brown is also pleasing. Larches are light in appearance and dark colours are not as good. The planting will probably begin life in a long seed tray, about 52.5 x 30 x 6.25cm (21 x 12 x 2½in). When the roots have grown together enough to hold position, the group can be transferred to the final pot.

Mosses

METHOD

Assemble this group in early spring, as the buds swell and are just splitting.

Work only with trees that have been root-established for a year at least. In this project, the grid is an important tool, as larch roots have great resilience and need careful coaxing into position.

Pre-wire and shape the trunks and branches. Use the 'temporary assemblage' technique, grouping the trunks as you style them. The group works by combining lines from two clumps as a canopy with a double spire, like a spiky letter 'M' – if you think of arrangements in this way it makes them seem familiar, less daunting and more achievable! It also helps you to analyse the design and work out why you like something, then to understand the shape and to make it work for you.

You need to know about the temporary container you are going to use. Plastic is fine as long as you appreciate that there is no porosity and that it does not breathe. This means you must watch the amounts of water you give and should stand the tray on a well-ventilated surface: if plastic sits on a solid shelf it makes an airtight seal and water is trapped there. Prepare the grid so it is an easy fit in the tray and pass location wires through the mesh.

Unpot the trees and root prune them lightly so that they are more easily combed out. Remove any heavy lower roots. Spread all the surface roots – you can even wire them out straight if they keep springing back on you! Remember to cut the wire after a month. Keep them damp.

The tallest tree (1) is placed on the left of the grid quite close to the edge, but located far enough from it to avoid binding on the container when planted. The tree will need a clearance of about 7.5cm (3in) and will look better standing just behind the major axis line. Secure it just firmly enough so that it does not topple and mess up your arrangement!

Look carefully at the other trees in the left-hand group. There is another tall trunk (2) behind the main tree on the right. The main tree overlaps it slightly, adding interest to the placement. Put that in next. There are two minor trunks to the left of the main tree (3, 4). Place these next

'M'-shaped arrangement of the trees.

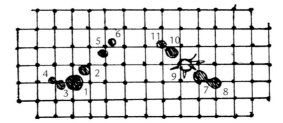

Tree placement.

and make sure they find root space in the front left area. Bigger trees can crowd out these little fellows. Secure them and arrange the branches of the outer tree to reinforce the image of a tiny foreground tree. There are two minor trunks (5, 6) behind and to the right of the main tree that complete the left-hand unit of the group. These are slightly removed from the main tree and their lines swing to the right. Their canopy crowns terminate at about one-third of the height of the main tree. They are standing on a low mound of soil that lifts their bases above that of the main tree. This means lifting them as they are placed and pouring more soil under them before twist-tying, so it will have to wait until the grid is secured in the container.

Now check the placement of everything. The trunk bases should form a diagonal line back to the right. Adjust and shift things around if necessary to achieve the correct position, as this suggests distance and depth.

The tallest tree in the right-hand group (7+8) has a double trunk and is placed roughly one-quarter of the way from the right-hand edge along the major axis and forward of it. Place this tree first and secure it so that it will not topple. Its crown terminates about three-quarters of the way up the height of the main tree on the left. The other three trunks are placed behind and to the left of the tall, twin-trunked tree. The trunk nearest the twin is quite heavy (9; I have stripped it as a dead tree) and the other

two are thinner (10, 11) but positioned so snugly together that they borrow from each other, giving the illusion of thickness. They are planted higher than the foreground trees and will be raised when planted in the container. Twist-tie them now so that they stand in position.

Check the overall placement. The trunk bases to the right should form a diagonal line back to the left. Adjust and play with the fine angles and positions until you are confident that it all works together. Now raise and feature as many surface roots as you can. Firm up the ties and get ready to transfer the grid to the container. Prepare the temporary container with drainage mesh, location wires and bottom soil. Lower and site the grid, and then tie it in position.

Add soil, making sure every face of the roots is penetrated and covered. Lift the back trees and pack soil beneath their roots so that they rise away from the grid. When they are at the required height, twist-tie the roots to the grid and the trees will hold their new elevation. Water in and saturate, and place the moss, leaving some root lines exposed. Water again lightly and make sure the moss is bedded well at the edges. Shade the group.

Bend, shape, trim and adjust the two profiles of the planting, keeping the left-hand side clearly taller. The negative spaces along the twin diagonals are great to play with, as are the different heights of the horizontal foliage masses. Look, for instance, at how the lowest point on the right-hand edge is high enough for the tiny tree on the left-hand edge to fit right under it! Thinking backwards and forwards through the design helps you to refine it and to develop details.

'yatsubusa' japanese maple

MULTI-TRUNK ROOT-CONNECTED GROUP
(See page 26)

COMPONENTS

'Yatsubusa' Japanese maple Source: bonsai and specialist maple nurseries should have stock of this cultivar. It is a vigorous tree with small green leaves and reddish spring growth. Get a 'busy' plant if possible.

Training wire For detailing the tree, use aluminium wire, 1mm and 1.5mm gauges.

Tools and sundries Wire cutters, branch pruners, trimming shears, rake, wound sealant, scalpel, hormone rooting powder, sphagnum moss soaked in vitamin B1 solution, clear and black polythene sheeting, rubber friction pads.

Container Temporary container, such as a long seed tray, prepared with drainage mesh, location wires and soil.

METHOD

Assemble this landscape in very early spring, as the buds swell.

Cut off the main trunk above a whorl of branches and seal the cut. Train the whorled branches out sideways. The original tree had a single base line, but yours can have more by training the branches out radially. Now layer the trunk.

Cut a double ring girdling the trunk, just below the branches. Make sure you cut through the outer bark and place the cuts about 2.5cm (1in) apart. Peel off the bark and dust the area with hormone rooting powder. Wrap the wrung-out, moistened sphagnum moss generously around the peeled area and tie it loosely in position. Wrap

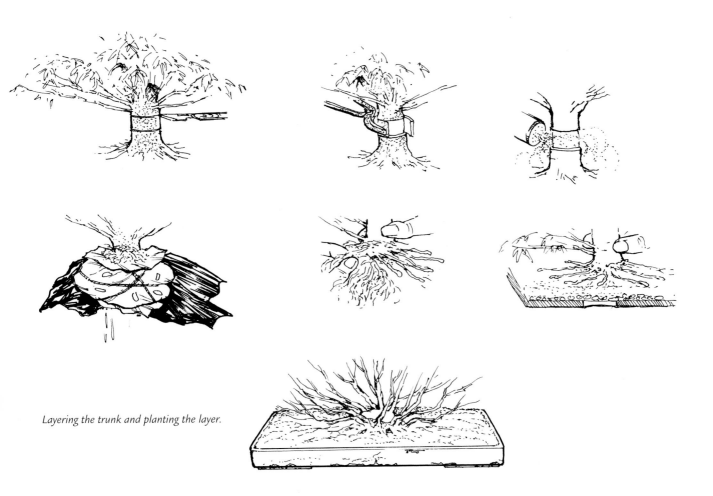

Layering the trunk and planting the layer.

again with clear polythene sheet and tie this around the tree above and below the mossed area to enclose it. Then wrap again with the black polythene.

Roots should appear after about a month. Unwrap the black polythene and check for root tips. When the new roots have grown through the moss and are lengthening, the layer can be detached from the old trunk, cutting it well below the rooted point, but first remove the wires on the branches.

Before you plant the layer, trim bark windows under the branches and dust them with hormone rooting powder. Gently unwrap the clear plastic and tease away the moss. Stop if roots break – they will snap like bean sprouts at this stage! Plant the layer in the temporary container, spread the roots gently and twist-tie over the branch lines, putting a friction pad over them. Add more soil and cover the spread branches. Tap the side of the pot to settle the soil. Water in well and shade the layer/root-connected maple. Feed once a month with 0–10–10 from midsummer to early autumn.

After about three years you will have a fine root-connected maple that will not be too far behind the original tree as it came from Japan.

Root-connected maple. If you allow the growth to extend to the periphery indicated by the arrows, you will achieve a beautiful form.

'catlin' elm

33-TRUNK GROVE
(See page 29)

COMPONENTS

33 catlin elms Height: 20–60cm (8–24in). Source: bonsai nurseries. It is unlikely you will find tall trunks, so get what you can that are suitable for groups and develop them for branching and sympathetic styling. Use shallow pots.

Training wire Thick enough to bend the trunks, probably 2–3mm aluminium. For detailing the trees, use 1mm and 1.5mm gauges.

Tools and sundries Wire cutters, branch pruners, trimming shears, rake, wound sealant, soil mix, plant location grid, drainage mesh.

Slab Size: 75 x 45 x 3.75cm (30 x 18 x 1½in) thick. Prepare a slab using the ciment fondu technique (see Chapter 6). Make a sunken planting area so that the edges will contain the roots and soil. Add drainage holes as you make the slab. Plant the elms in a low container that will fit into the planting zone.

Mosses

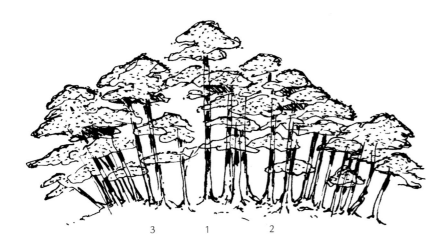

Arrangement of the trees.

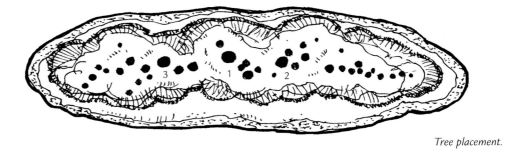

Tree placement.

METHOD

Assemble this group in spring, as the buds swell.

Pre-wire the trunks and branches and bend them so that the shapes are gently undulating. Prepare the inner container that will fit inside the planting area with drainage mesh, location wires and a good layer of soil. Unpot the trees, then comb out and trim the roots. Keep them damp.

Place the tallest tree (1) to the left of the centre and back from the major axis, and loosely twist-tie it so that it will not topple. Place the next tallest trunks to the right and left (2, 3), and then cluster the remaining trunks around those three points. Remember to use thicks and thins. Angle the trunks so that they gradually move outwards from a point near the tallest tree. Add smaller trunks at the edges on the left and to the rear. Make the soil mound into two low hills and lift the trees so that they sit naturally on them. Emphasize surface roots to encourage trunk flare.

Check the effect from a distance. You will probably want to adjust the lateral placement to form those lovely negative areas. When you are satisfied with the trees' posture and placement, twist-tie everything firmly. Adjust, prune, bend and shape the canopies for the billowing contours. Open dense areas to introduce negative space throughout the branches and their trunk junctions. One obvious adjustment that has been made here is the way in which the horizontal negative area above the soil line begins low on the left, suddenly widens by the main tree, then thins again and finally lifts the canopy at the right-hand edge. If you do not achieve it in one go, it will come – remember that the original took 25 years!

Place the container in the slab and add soil to cover the rim only. Add moss across the whole surface of the planting and water in well. Shade the group.

It is worth repeating that the exquisite tracery seen here was developed without much nitrogen.

'san josé' juniper

PROJECT 12

THREE-TRUNK SAIKEI
(See page 30)

COMPONENTS

Three 'San José' junipers Height: 25cm, 45cm and 55cm (10in, 18in and 22in). Source: bonsai nurseries offer a good range of pre-bonsai examples of this popular species, where the trunks and branches are already roughly styled and it is easy to grow them into something better. Select three trunks ranging in size from thumb to little-finger thickness. Garden centres also carry the trees and they are easily trained.

Training wire Thick enough to bend the trunks, probably 2.5–3mm aluminium. For detailing the trees, use 1mm, 1.5mm and 2mm gauges.

Tools and sundries Wire cutters, branch pruners, trimming shears, rake, wound sealant, soil mix, drainage mesh.

Container Oval. Size: 70 x 50 x 4.5cm (28 x 20 x 1¾in). Colour: brown unglazed.

Rocks Five grey rocks, one about 30cm (12in) high and 7.5cm (3in) wide, the others much smaller.

Sand Light grey and brown fine sand.

Mosses, ferns and dwarf mondo grasses

METHOD

Assemble this group in spring.

Pre-wire and shape the three trunks and branches so that all the lines flow and work together well. Prepare the container with drainage mesh, location wires and bottom soil. Unpot the trees and comb out and trim the roots. Place the main tree (1) in the pot about 22.5cm (9in) from the left-hand edge and well to the back. Tilt the tree to the right and place the tall rock beside and slightly in front of it. Place the smallest tree (2) 12.5cm (5in) from the right-hand edge and well to the back. Place the third tree (3) halfway between edge of the rock and the small tree, also well to the back. Add soil and make sure the roots are well permeated and covered. Twist-tie the trees into position. Bed the rock in well so that it rises naturally. Mound and contour the soil to make an elliptical island with a level foreground.

Tree placement.

Add the other rocks. There is a small one to the left of the big tree and the others are placed below and to the right of the standing stone. Bed them in and add the mondo grasses and ferns. Add smaller mounds of soil in the foreground to suggest banks. Saturate with water, place the mosses and water everything in well. Place the sand. Use the light grey in the foreground between the banks and the brown sand along the edge of the planting beneath the mondo grass. Shade the landscape.

Check everything and adjust branch details. Look carefully at the length and angles of the branches. You will notice that the lower side of the first left-hand branch forms a line with the lowest part of the higher-placed middle tree. The little tree on the right is small enough to fit under the line and its main thrust swings down to the right. Have fun with it!

trident maple

11-TRUNK RAFT GROUP
(See page 32)

COMPONENTS

Trident maple Source: bonsai nurseries should have some wiggly-trunked, low-quality trident maples among their imports that provide an excellent start for a raft. I have started a number like this and it works very well. Get as fat a trunk as you can, but try not to pay 'specimen tree' money – you only need a curvy trunk, not a great tree.

Training wire For detailing the branches, use aluminium wire, 1.5mm, 2mm and 2.5mm gauges.

Tools and sundries Wire cutters, branch pruners, trimming shears, rake, wound sealant, scalpel, rooting hormone powder, rubber friction pads.

Container Temporary container such as a long seed tray prepared with drainage mesh, location wires and soil.

METHOD

Assemble this landscape in spring, as the buds swell and split.

Tilt the potted trunk right over and check it for the best line. Pre-wire the branches on the upper side and prune those on the lower side. Cut bark windows with a scalpel. Peel the bark flaps away and treat the exposed area with hormone rooting powder.

Unpot the tree and comb out the roots. Prune away about half the mass of roots that will point upwards as the trunk is laid over. Lay the trunk in the pot, spreading the lower roots along the trunk. Place the upper ones so that they sit as flat as possible.

Place friction pads on the upper trunk and twist-tie it into position with the location wires. Add more soil, making sure all the root faces are permeated and covered. Shade the tree. Bend, place and style the branch/trunk lines. Stand the pot on blocks for air circulation. Level off the soil and water in well.

For full details of the technique and diagrams, see page 70.

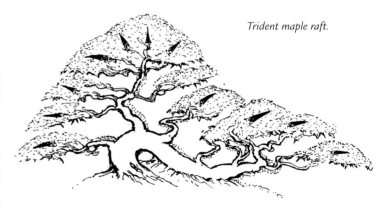

Trident maple raft.

AFTERCARE

Feeding
After a month, feed with half-strength Miracle-Gro every two weeks. In midsummer switch to 0–10–10 once a month until early autumn.

Follow the system adopted for developing the original tree for about five years (see page 33–35) and you will have a superb tree.

tree care directory

For details of the soil components, wound sealants, insecticides and other items mentioned in the Directory, plus general watering, feeding and maintenance advice, see Chapters 2 and 4.

BEECH (European, Japanese White)

Fagus sylvatica, F. crenata

HABITAT AND PLACEMENT

Beech is a woodland species that is very adaptable and can be found growing as a huge tree in the plains, or as a dwarfed, shrubby specimen in the mountains. It will prosper in a variety of soils and in the UK grows on chalky or acid soil. As bonsai and in the miniature landscape, beech like a shaded position – they are soon scorched in the sun.

TRUNK

The bark of the young European beech ages to a light silver-grey, while that of the Japanese tree becomes white and lustrous. It is important to know that beech scar hugely and if any branch removal is planned, it is better to do this at the end of the growing season. Sometimes, rather than taking the branch at the base, the stump is left unpruned and as it dies back, the bark around the base forms a ring rather than a big lump of callus. The stump can be removed after a year or two and should heal fairly flat.

SOIL

This is a tree that enjoys free-draining soil. It does well in a mixture of half sand and half light organic material. In Europe, a mix that works well is 5 parts mixed sand, 3 parts ericaceous compost, 1 part leaf mould and 1 part peat.

POTTING AND REPOTTING

When potting up raw stock, use a medium-depth container for a year in order to build a shallow root pad. Repot every three to four years, as the buds swell. If a change of container is indicated, do not use anything too shallow: the trees like cool roots and are easily leaf scorched. Once established, beech form a fairly shallow root pad – you will often see a beech blown over after a gale and mature trees on chalk, for instance, often have a rootball that is no deeper than 90–120cm (3–4ft). Once in a pot, beech need shade and water to stay green and flourishing.

WATERING

Keep beech damp; they like regular watering. Do not let them dry out – ever. Mist the leaves after they have set to keep the tree happy (leaves are 'set' when they feel leathery). If you mist the leaves prior to leaf set, you can expect foliage the size of cabbage leaves!

FEEDING

Beech enjoy nitrogen, but will also coarsen rapidly if they get too much, so give it early in the year. Switch to a low-nitrogen feed and taper that off by midsummer. Finish by giving a feed that is rich in potash and phosphorus. A typical programme is: Miracid at half strength every two weeks during spring; Fish Emulsion every two weeks through until midsummer; 0–10–10 monthly from late summer to mid-autumn.

TRIMMING

Soft extending growth is pinched back when the leaves can be seen. They uncurl in a soft, downy mass and you need to take care to remove just the terminal leaves from the shoots. Branches are pruned in late summer/early autumn. I find that early-autumn pruning produced the best results, as there is enough growing time left to promote a little healing, but without the unsightly, lumpy calluses provoked by mid-year pruning. Seal cuts with a wound compound.

WIRING

Wire beech in midsummer using aluminium training wire. Shade the trees after wiring. Check routinely for wires biting into wood and remove tight ones promptly – beech can grow so fast that they become wire-bitten in a couple of weeks! De-wire in autumn before the first frost.

PESTS

Mealy bug can be a pest on new growth. A systemic spray will usually take care of the problem.

DISEASES

Substantially free.

STYLING

Formal, broom, informal, group, raft and root-connected.

BOX

Buxus species

HABITAT AND PLACEMENT

Box is an evergreen shrub to small tree. It is very adaptable and is found in the southern UK, Africa, North America, Asia and Europe. There are lots of different varieties and some are very dwarf. It is a versatile plant but likes dappled shade.

TRUNK

The bark of mature box is a yellowy white and that at the base of the trunk is often divided into flaky plates. Young plants appear green for the most part; older plants look attractive with the maturing pale bark contrasting with their roundish, dark green leaves.

SOIL

The soil mixture recommended for beech also suits box.

POTTING AND REPOTTING

Use medium-depth containers. Box trees like a poor soil in nature, but one that is free draining and moist. When repotting any of the box species, do not reduce the roots too drastically in one go – always go halfway for a year, as it is the sudden withdrawal of moisture that does the damage. Repot every three years as the buds swell. Shade the tree after repotting.

WATERING

Give plenty of water. Misting the leaves is a big help, as is placing the plant in dappled shade.

FEEDING

Box enjoy food, but be careful not to give too much nitrogen as the trees can thicken and coarsen rapidly. A typical programme is: Miracle-Gro at half strength every two weeks in spring; Fish Emulsion once a month in summer; 0–10–10 once a month from late summer to mid-autumn.

TRIMMING

Pinch new growth back to two leaves. Avoid letting growth extend too far, as the shoots rapidly become thick. Branches are pruned in autumn and, as with beech, early autumn is the best period. The cuts should be sealed with a wound compound, as this promotes budding – unsealed wood often becomes so dry that buds are not produced.

WIRING

Wire box in the summer and de-wire again before the frosts, or keep the plants frost free over the winter. Use aluminium training wire and apply the thinnest that will do the job. Avoid tight wires as box can be sensitive to metal contact. The wood is brittle and splits at forks.

PESTS

Scale insects and mealy bug are the main pests. Use a systemic insecticide.

DISEASES

Substantially free.

STYLING

Informal, group, raft and root connected.

CEDAR (Japanese)

Cryptomeria japonica

HABITAT AND PLACEMENT

This large, upright-growing, evergreen tree is a native of shaded foothills and does well in light woodland. As a bonsai or in miniature landscape, cryptomerias are definite candidates for dappled shade. They soon become crisped in full sun and once soft tissue dries out, budding is poor.

TRUNK

The bark of mature trees is reddish brown and flaky, and it becomes thick with age. The trunk remains very active and will sprout shoots and aerial roots if conditions are damp.

SOIL

Cryptomerias like a well-drained soil that retains some moisture and a good mix is 5 parts mixed sand, 3 parts composted peat and 2 parts leaf mould.

POTTING AND REPOTTING

For single bonsai, do not use anything too shallow for the main root mass. In the landscape with rocks and contoured soil, a lot of moisture is retained and a shallow root run is less of a problem. When potting down from the general nursery large plastic pot, carry out the operation in two stages and run the tree for a year in an intermediate-sized pot to avoid causing it stress. Cryptomerias can be weak and they do not appreciate sudden drops in their moisture supply. Repot every two to four years, according to age and vigour, and after repotting place the trees in dappled shade and spray the leaves. Repot from early to late spring, but avoid cold weather.

WATERING

Give plenty of water on the roots and leaves, but ventilate well and make sure the water does not puddle under the pot. Aim for a steady dampness.

FEEDING

Feed with Miracle-Gro at half strength every two weeks from early spring to late summer, alternating with Fish Emulsion. Switch to monthly doses of 0–10–10 from early to mid-autumn.

TRIMMING

Pinch back soft growth when it is thumbnail length. Use a light twisting motion rather than a deep fingernail gouge. The shoot should retain some needles after shortening. This procedure keeps the moisture level up and preserves budding as a result. Branches are removed in late spring. It is a good idea to seal the cuts. Periodically, the foliage will need thinning to admit light and air. If the leaf density is not reduced, foliage can dry up and there may be extensive die-back. Thinning is carried out in summer.

WIRING

Wire in warm weather – late spring is a good time, when all danger of frost has passed. Use aluminium wire and wire only brown wood, as immature green wood dislikes this procedure intensely. It is possible to carry out detailed wiring if you remember to wire the main branches first and then just enough length on the side branches to give

control. The final detailing comes from fine pinching of new growth.

PESTS

Substantially free.

DISEASES

Cryptomerias sometimes get reddened areas of foliage in excessively wet conditions. Improved ventilation and lighter soil will help, while copper fungicide will take care of the symptoms. Do not mistake the winter colour, which is purplish, for the red of the blight.

STYLING

Formal, group, raft and root connected.

COTONEASTER

C. horizontalis and other species

HABITAT AND PLACEMENT

Cotoneaster horizontalis has been in cultivation in the UK for over a hundred years. It is well adapted to growing over walls and rockeries – hence the common name rockspray. *C. horizontalis* is deciduous, but if you want an evergreen plant there are several species, such as *C. microphyllus*, that are just as adaptable in use and placement. Once potted, keep cotoneasters in dappled shade.

TRUNK

The bark becomes silver-brown with age. *C. horizontalis* has the advantage of being a strong grower but one that is fairly easily controlled. This means that you can generate a nice thick trunk and still keep the branches under control if you prune adequately. The trunk form is multi-stemmed with a shallow arching habit.

SOIL

Cotoneasters will grow in many different soils in open ground, but once potted they like a light but rich organic mixture, such as 3 parts composted peat, 2 parts akadama, 3 parts leaf mould and 2 parts mixed sand.

POTTING AND REPOTTING

Cotoneasters are repotted as the buds swell. Plants in a landscape situation can be root-pruned every three to four years, depending on root-run. If the root-run is small, repot every two to three years. Cotoneasters are tough and can tolerate a lot of root reduction if they are healthy, but if the roots are not good for some reason (such as when initially working with container stock that may have tight and neglected roots) transplant them without too much root disturbance, using the suggested well-drained soil mix. There should then be a rapid improvement. The root mass can be reduced at the next repotting.

WATERING

Keep cotoneasters damp – they like water. Misting the leaves is beneficial.

FEEDING

Feed when the leaves swell until the flowering period. Give Miracle-Gro at half strength every two weeks, alternating with 0–10–10. After flowering, substitute Fish Emulsion for Miracle-Gro and resume alternate feeds until late summer. Do not feed in hot weather to avoid triggering coarse growth. From late summer to mid-autumn feed monthly with 0–10–10.

TRIMMING

Branches are pruned in late spring. New soft growth can be trimmed closely, keeping a pair of leaves; or it can be allowed to extend to fill a gap; or it may be removed entirely, as suits the design.

WIRING

Wire new growth in early summer using aluminium training wire. Older wood is hard – sometimes very hard – and may need to be cut back rather than risking any splits and breaks through the heavy pressure that is needed to bend it.

PESTS

Aphids and scale insects are the most prevalent pests. Treat them with an oil-based spray such as Volck rather than with systemic insecticides.

DISEASES

Substantially free. Can occasionally get some tar spots on the leaves if ventilation is poor. Treat with copper fungicide.

STYLING

All the styles are suitable for cotoneasters. They look superb as rock-grown plants.

CYPRESS (Sawara)

Chamaecyparis pisifera

HABITAT AND PLACEMENT

The Sawara cypress is native to Japan, where it inhabits the plains and foothills. It has been grown in the UK for over a hundred years and can make a large, upright tree. It has produced many cultivars and 'Tsukumo' (syn. 'Tsukumo-hiba') is one of the best. The trees thrive in dappled shade.

TRUNK

The short trunk of 'Tsukumo' thickens with age and often produces brown, flaky bark. The shape is typically short and multi-trunked.

SOIL

'Tsukumo' likes a well-drained soil that retains some moisture. The roots need to breathe and care should be taken to sieve the soil. A suitable mix is 5 parts mixed sand, 3 parts composted peat and 2 parts leaf mould.

POTTING AND REPOTTING

Repot every two years in early to mid-spring. The plant is pretty tough, and provided not too much root fibre is removed, it can take quite a significant reduction of soil mass if necessary for the design.

WATERING

Keep damp but not wringing wet. Misting the leaves is very beneficial.

FEEDING

Feed with Miracle-Gro at half strength, alternating with Fish Emulsion, every two weeks from early spring to late summer. From early to late autumn, feed with 0–10–10 once a month.

TRIMMING

Pinch soft tip growth only when it is long enough to trim easily with the fingernails: if you go deeper on new growth it often dies back. 'Tsukumo' grows in a diffuse way and pinching back is a continual process throughout the growing season. The results of pinching are a tightening of the foliage texture so that it becomes pleasingly dense and compact. Branches are pruned in early autumn. Seal any larger cuts with wound sealant.

WIRING

Wiring is seldom necessary with a plant that makes a rounded shape like this. Aluminium training wire can be used to correct wild shoots, branches and occasionally the trunk, but extensive work is not required.

PESTS

Substantially free.

DISEASES

Sometimes if the plant is kept very wet it can develop discoloured foliage zones that then die back. In these circumstances it will be found that the roots are also damaged. If such areas appear, check ventilation, watering and soil conditions. Prune away damaged foliage and treat the plant with copper fungicide.

STYLING

Because it is so short in stature, 'Tsukumo' is best styled very simply, so that it gives a feeling of, say, the formal or leaning styles or a group of trees, rather than by thinning it out too much. It looks superb with rocks and stones.

ELM (Chinese)

Ulmus parvifolia

HABITAT AND PLACEMENT

The Chinese elm grows in a wide distribution throughout China, Korea and Japan. Although mainly found on the plains, where it makes a medium-sized tree, it also grows in the foothills, although under these conditions it makes a shorter plant. As a bonsai, it does best in dappled shade and frost-free conditions. Keep the trees out of deep shade as this causes die-back.

TRUNK

Chinese elm and its cultivars are upright trees with interesting bark that varies from smooth and silver to rough, corky and deep brown.

SOIL

Chinese elms like a well-drained soil. The roots are fleshy and easily damaged, becoming prone to rot, but the right choice of soil can alleviate the problem, as it can change the nature of the root formation to some extent, making it finer and more wiry. A soil that works is 5 parts mixed sand, 3 parts composted peat and 2 parts leaf mould.

POTTING AND REPOTTING

Elms are repotted as the buds swell, usually in early spring, but Chinese elms can be very early. It is best to go by the tree. Repot young plants every year and older plants according to root production, about every two to four years. Remove old and thickened lower roots: it is always better to try to keep these trees producing finer roots, which appear to be less prone to injury. Keep the old cut roots – they can be used as cuttings and will soon sprout buds.

WATERING

Keep the trees damp. They like to breathe and require good air exchange through the soil. A lot of water/moisture balance may be provided safely through leaf misting.

FEEDING

Feed every two weeks from budding to shoot extension with half-strength Miracid. When the leaves are fully out, switch to Fish Emulsion, given once a month from midspring to early summer. Give 0–10–10 monthly from midsummer to early autumn.

TRIMMING

Pinch growth back whenever it has made three to four leaves. Any branch pruning or other major surgery is best done right at the end of the season (when the leaves fall) , when the wound healing mechanism is less efficient. This prevents swollen scar tissue from forming.

WIRING

Exercise care when wiring Chinese elms, as they can be extremely brittle. If older wood is to be bent, allow the tree to dry a little to relax the wood. Then, as you bend the coiled section, make sure you enclose it totally inside your linked hands and squeeze and bend together. Even old and brittle wood can be shaped if enough care is taken. However, normally wiring is confined to young wood that is more pliable and is carried out in midsummer. Always use aluminium wire.

PESTS

Aphids and scale insects are the main problems. Treat them with an oil-based spray such as Volck rather than with systemic insecticides.

DISEASES
Substantially free.

STYLING
All the styles are suitable for this very versatile plant.

HEMLOCK (Western, Eastern)

Tsuga heterophylla, T. canadensis

HABITAT AND PLACEMENT

Large, upright-growing, evergreen trees, hemlocks are native to fairly high terrain and so are used to exposure. Nevertheless, they appreciate some screening and grow lush in dappled shade.

TRUNK

In good conditions, the natural form is broadly conical and the trunk is tapered and straight. There are many dwarf and weeping forms. Hemlocks with very dwarfed and twisted trunk forms can be collected in tundra-like conditions in the northwestern US.

SOIL

The trees like a well-drained soil that retains some moisture, and a good mix is: 5 parts mixed sand, 3 parts composted peat and 2 parts leaf mould.

POTTING AND REPOTTING

Young trees can be root-pruned every three years or so, older trees less often – a lot depends on the amount of growth and the colour of the leaves. If growth is slow and the leaves are yellowy, this usually indicates dryness, most commonly caused by a tight root mass. Root pruning will correct this, but never take too much root fibre at one time. Repot in early to late spring. Hemlocks grow better in a medium to deep container.

WATERING

Keep the trees damp and mist the leaves. Be careful to avoid drought. Hemlocks are pretty trees and look best with deep green growth, and this is soon sacrificed if they are carelessly watered.

FEEDING

Feed with Miracle-Gro monthly from mid- to late spring. Feed with Fish Emulsion monthly from early to late summer. Finally, use 0–10–10 monthly from early to late autumn.

TRIMMING

Pinch out new soft growth, retaining some base needles. Growth is pruned back from early to midsummer until early autumn. Branches can be pruned during the growing season, the optimum period being early autumn.

WIRING

Some cultivars, notably the dwarf types, can be touchy about the season for wiring, and these are best wired early or late in the year to avoid disturbing new growth. Others are tougher and can take more abuse, but even so, do use aluminium wire to minimize the harshness of the metal contact.

PESTS

Substantially free.

DISEASES

Substantially free.

STYLING

Most of the suggested styles 'work' with hemlocks. They are very versatile plants in pot culture, and also extraordinary natural trunk forms can be found – with squat and convoluted trunks, combining an extreme 'S' bend with a raft form, and so on. So, you can allow the trees to be pretty much free form and the key when styling is, does it look right? The planes of the branches lend themselves to training and shaping and give superb results.

HORNBEAM

Carpinus betulus and other species

HABITAT AND PLACEMENT

The hornbeams are a picturesque group of trees with an attractive, meandering pattern of branches. They grow in Europe, Asia and North America and are hardy, being found in a wide variety of locations, even in high terrain. The species vary from upright to shrubby forms and all have interesting hop-like fruit clusters. They do best in dappled shade. An exciting collection can be built up by choosing from the many colours and sizes of leaves, bark textures and fruits offered by this lovely plant group.

TRUNK

The trunk is usually upright and the trees develop considerable vertical 'fluting' or fissured indenting as they age, giving them an interesting geometric structure. The bark is light grey, often striped with buff.

SOIL

Use a mixture of 5 parts mixed light organic material such as peat and leaf mould, 2 parts akadama and 3 parts mixed sand.

POTTING AND REPOTTING

Never under-pot hornbeams: even in Japan you will see them in shallow containers suffering from leaf scorch. Go for a medium depth, or if you must have 'shallow', mound the soil to conserve water. Repot in spring with the swelling of the buds. Repot every other year, or less often with older trees and those in large landscape settings.

WATERING

Hornbeams need water and rapidly become leaf scorched without adequate moisture. They appreciate their leaves being misted in the evening.

FEEDING

Alternate half-strength Miracle-Gro with Fish Emulsion every two weeks from bud break until early summer. Feed with 0–10–10 monthly from midsummer to early autumn.

TRIMMING

Whenever new growth extends over three leaves, trim back to two. Older branches are pruned in early autumn. Seal cuts with Lac-Balsam, as its colour blends well with the bark.

WIRING

Hornbeams burn easily when hot sun warms up the wire, so use aluminium wire and shade the tree after wiring. Midsummer is the best time to do this. Old wood is very hard and almost unbendable, but younger growth is easily wired.

PESTS

Aphids can be a problem. Treat them with an oil-based spray such as Volck rather than with systemic insecticides.

DISEASES

Substantially free.

STYLING

All the styles are suitable for hornbeams.

JUNIPER (Chinese)

Juniperus chinensis, J. x media

HABITAT AND PLACEMENT

Chinese junipers are evergreens of variable form, ranging from upright trees and shrubs to prostrate plants. They grow in high terrain in the Himalayas, China and Japan. As potted plants, they prefer dappled shade.

TRUNK

Those used in bonsai (see page 50) are often multi-trunked and sometimes prostrate. The bark is shaggy and dark brown on young plants, maturing to a thicker, reddish, smoother bark. The wood hardens as it ages.

SOIL

Junipers prefer good drainage, and a mixture of 5 parts mixed sand, 3 parts leaf mould and 2 parts akadama will supply the needs of most types. Avoid peat in this instance, as junipers like a neutral or alkaline soil. In the UK, the native junipers do well on chalky soil.

POTTING AND REPOTTING

Chinese junipers prefer cool roots. This means that even old trees need regular root pruning every three years or so. As with most evergreens, profoundly old trees are repotted much less often. Younger trees in smaller pots need regular attention to avoid their roots forming a 'horse's-collar' of pot-encircling outer roots. These are the roots that get scorched if the pot warms up in sunlight. The root collar should be cut off, and the roots combed out and trimmed to even them. This will restore the balance of vigour. Repot in early to mid-spring.

WATERING

Junipers enjoy dampness but dislike soggy conditions. For example, when *J. communis* is found in a wet spot, it often has an upper and lower root system. The bottom set anchors the tree and the upper set supplies the oxygen. When such a tree is collected, planted in open soil and shaded, the leaves open and flourish and the plant prospers. So, if you think of a tree growing in mountain scree, with fast drainage and cloud cover supplying humidity, you can reproduce the perfect watering, with a damp soil and foliage misting combined with placement in dappled shade. After any root disturbance, do not mist the leaves for a week or two as they need to express moisture rapidly.

FEEDING

Feed every week with half-strength Miracle-Gro from early spring to late summer. Give 0–10–10 once a month from early to mid-autumn.

TRIMMING

Pinch new growth tips when they are long enough to take with the soft part of thumb and forefinger. Chinese juniper grows in a diffuse way and the pinching triggers side buds, so this is a continuing process through the year. Do not prune too much of the tree at one session. Prune old branches in early autumn.

WIRING

Wire at any time, but avoid frost contact if wired in winter. After wiring, shade the plants and mist the foliage. Old wood is hard and wiring is best done on young growth up to pencil thickness.

PESTS

Look for red spider. A natural way to foil this lover of dry conditions is by misting the foliage. Attacks are best treated with a contact insecticide such as malathion, or with an emulsion-type spray such as Volck.

DISEASES

Substantially free.

STYLING

All the styles are suitable for Chinese junipers.

LARCH (Japanese, European)

Larix leptolepis, L. decidua

HABITAT AND PLACEMENT

These larches are widely distributed in Europe. Both the Japanese and European types are adaptable and have produced the hybrid Dunkeld larch (*Larix x eurolepis*), also a winner in the miniature landscape. As bonsai and in the miniature landscape, they need light shade and can take a fair amount of frost.

TRUNK

The young bark of the Japanese tree is orangey, maturing to purple. The young bark of the European tree tends towards a yellowy colour, maturing to grey. Older trees of both species have similar grey bark with fissures.

SOIL

Larches like a well-drained soil, and a good mix is 5 parts mixed sand, 2 parts leaf mould and 3 parts peat.

POTTING AND REPOTTING

It is important to repot every two to three years, and older trees every three to four years. If the intervening periods are any longer, horrendous die-back can follow, with whole branches becoming desiccated and dying. If the roots are kept active through repotting, livelier trees will result. Larches may be a little touchy after repotting before their roots take hold. Repot in early to mid-spring, as the buds swell and the first green shows.

WATERING

Keep larches damp. They do best in dappled shade and like their roots to be cool. After the leaves have set their length in summer, the trees appreciate foliage misting.

FEEDING

Give 0–10–10 twice when the new shoots appear, at two-week intervals in early spring. Switch to half-strength Miracle-Gro every two weeks from mid-spring to early summer. Give Fish Emulsion every two weeks from mid- to late summer. If you keep the nitrogen down as suggested, the branches tend to stay slim. Otherwise, they can easily coarsen and outgrow the overall scale.

TRIMMING

Pinch/prune back new growth when it extends beyond 5cm (2in). Periodically, the trees will need thinning out to avoid an over-heavy appearance. They are very willing to bud. When thinning and grooming, remove inner growth close to the trunk line and any hanging or ascending lines. This will tidy, open and lighten the trees. Old branches are removed in early autumn.

WIRING

Wire in late summer or early autumn. Keep wired trees frost free. De-wire the following year in late summer. Maintain a careful watch for wires biting in, as larch wood expands fast and the trees can quickly become scarred.

PESTS

Substantially free.

DISEASES

Substantially free.

STYLING

All the styles are suitable for larches.

MAPLE (Japanese)

Acer palmatum

HABITAT AND PLACEMENT

Japanese maples grow widely throughout Japan, central China and Korea. They enjoy light woodland with dappled shade and a slightly acidic soil.

TRUNK

The trunk is variable with most forms as uprights, but there are weeping plants and many dwarf types. The young growth is light green, ageing to buff and light grey. The trees are often multi-trunked and spreading.

SOIL

A light, well-drained soil works best with potted trees. In open ground they can take a heavier soil, but in the potted landscape use a mix of 5 parts sand, 1 part akadama, 2 parts leaf mould and 2 parts composted peat.

POTTING AND REPOTTING

Japanese maples are repotted as the buds swell in early to mid-spring, and less commonly in summer after the leaves are trimmed off. Repot young plants every two years, older plants every three to four years. If you break this schedule, the trees often weaken and fail to grow well.

WATERING

Japanese maples like water. Keep them damp, not soggy. After the leaves have set their size in summer, misting the foliage in the evening is beneficial in warm weather.

FEEDING

Feed every two weeks from budding-out to early summer with half-strength Miracle-Gro. From mid- to late summer give Fish Emulsion every two weeks. Give 0–10–10 once a month from early to mid-autumn.

TRIMMING

Pinch or prune back to two leaves after new growth has made about three to four pairs of leaves. Any large individual leaves can be trimmed off any time that they go oversize during the growing season. Gradually they will be replaced with finer foliage, which will produce finer twigs as well. The leaves become very dense and will need periodic grooming and thinning. Remove growth close to the trunk, any dangling leaves below the branch line and any new ascending shoot lines – these three simple steps will open up and refine the trees quite profoundly. If they still look heavy, check for opposite shoot lines and prune away one pair, alternating left and right. The trees will soon appear considerably lighter.

WIRING

Wire in summer and always use soft aluminium training wire – maples have sensitive bark that detests metal. Keep a careful watch to make sure there is no biting in: wire-bitten maples will be ruined until eventually the scars grow out. De-wire as soon as the wires look tight.

PESTS

Aphids and scale insects are the worst offenders. Treat them with an oil-based spray such as Volck rather than with systemic insecticides.

DISEASES

Mildews, both wet and dry, affect maples. Attend to ventilation and spray with a broad-spectrum fungicide. Coral spot is sometimes found on old rotted tissue in wet conditions. Cut out the damaged tissue and burn it. Paint the wound with fungicide and seal the cut.

STYLING

All the styles are suitable for Japanese maples.

MAPLE (Trident)

Acer buergerianum

HABITAT AND PLACEMENT

Trident maples are distributed throughout eastern China and Japan. They like light woodland with dappled shade and an acidic soil.

TRUNK

The trunk is upright and the trees are of small to medium size, like Japanese maples. The young bark is light green, ageing to buff and grey. As it ages, the bark breaks off in plates, exposing an orange underbark. Later, the bark darkens to dark grey.

SOIL

Trident maples grow best in a light soil as they have fleshy roots: a mixture of 5 parts mixed sand, 2 parts leaf mould and 3 parts composted peat will work well and encourage the formation of finer roots.

POTTING AND REPOTTING

Repot in spring when the buds swell. It is important to repot young trident maples every year and older trees every two to three years – they are prolific root producers and the pot soon becomes choked, leading to further deterioration of the roots as water and air fail to penetrate the mass. (I once had the job of repotting a very old plant that had been neglected for so long that the 'horse's collar' of girdling roots under the soil was formed by a square, pot-shaped main root 5cm (2in) thick that was so old it had mature bark. Luckily, the pot was so massive that even after this was sawn off in logs, the inner roots were found still to be active – but it was not a happy situation!)

WATERING

Trident maples enjoy water, but avoid keeping the soil soggy at all costs. The favourite combination of damp soil, dappled shade and leaf misting works best.

FEEDING

Follow the schedule for Japanese maples.

TRIMMING

Follow the schedule for Japanese maples. Trident maples are more vigorous than Japanese maples and like to produce lots of vertical shoots. They will therefore need a lot of grooming to maintain and develop the shape, but soon become mature and beautiful as a result of your work!

WIRING

Follow the schedule for Japanese maples. Be extra vigilant in watching for wire biting – these are strong-growing trees that can swell up at an alarming rate.

PESTS

Aphids and scale insects. Treat them with an oil-based spray such as Volck rather than with systemic insecticides.

DISEASES

Mildew and tar spot can be a problem, but both can be treated with fungicide. Improve ventilation and keep water off the foliage. Some leaf thinning may be necessary to prevent heavy leaf masses sticking together and encouraging fresh outbreaks.

STYLING

All the styles are suitable for trident maples.

PINE (Scots)

Pinus sylvestris and cultivars

HABITAT AND PLACEMENT

Scots pines are very widely distributed from Europe to Siberia and in North America. They can take a range of different environments and are very hardy. The trees prefer a sandy, lightly acidic soil. For the best colour, grow potted plants in dappled shade.

TRUNK

The trunk of the wildling is usually upright and older trees shed their lower branches and form a typical parasol-topped silhouette. The thinner upper bark is salmon-pink blending down to deep purple-grey, with fissured, thickly corked bark plates on the lower trunk. The form is variable and there are many dwarf garden forms in cultivation.

SOIL

Scots pines prefer a light, well-drained soil. They enjoy rapid drainage, so a mixture of 5 parts mixed sand, 3 parts composted peat and 2 parts leaf mould, with perhaps some healthy, well-rotted dead needles added to it, will suit the trees. The old needles introduce beneficial fungal activity to the soil.

POTTING AND REPOTTING

Repot every three to five years as the buds swell in early to mid-spring. If the trees are repotted more frequently they tend to grow out of shape and produce huge needles.

WATERING

Keep the trees damp. Scots pines like water but do not keep them soggy. Placement in dappled shade will conserve moisture and this means less frequent watering will be required. This in turn really helps to keep new leaves from growing too long – a major problem with pines.

FEEDING

Feed with Miracid as a foliar feed once a month from midwinter to early spring. This brings the colour up and invigorates the tree. From mid- to late spring soil feed with half-strength Miracle-Gro every two weeks. Discontinue feeding from early to midsummer, then recommence with one feed of Fish Emulsion. Give 0–10–10 once a month from late summer to mid-autumn.

TRIMMING

New shoots extend by late spring and will be of uneven length. The first step is to cut down the longest shoots to match the length of the medium ones. By early to mid-summer the shoots will have hardened off. All growth that exceeds 2.5cm (1in) in length is then pruned at the base. Do not prune the weakest shoots. This makes for greater bud/shoot activity and denser needles. In autumn, reduce the number of resting terminal buds to two. In winter, trim the inner needles to admit light and air and to refine the appearance. Prune old branches in early autumn. If back budding is required, trim the terminals in late summer. Buds form between the needles and pop out on old wood. Once the new buds make needles, the terminals may be shortened again. The buds can get very dense and may need thinning out.

WIRING

Use aluminium training wire and wire the trees in late summer to early autumn. Watch out for it biting in – Scots pines can take off like a rocket and the wood swells quickly. De-wire after a year, or before the wire looks tight.

PESTS

Woolly aphids and mealy bugs are the main problems and both can be controlled with a systemic insecticide like dimethoate or a contact spray like malathion. The oil emulsion spray Volck is also excellent.

DISEASES

Needle cast is the worst problem. Look for gold spangles and dots on the needles, and remove and burn any that are affected – kicking them under the bench is not enough! Spray with copper fungicide or one containing zineb, during warm weather when the disease is most active. This will arrest the condition.

STYLING

Formal, informal, leaning and group styles all suit Scots pines very well.

SPRUCE (Alberta)

Picea glauca var. *albertiana*

HABITAT AND PLACEMENT

This dwarf form of spruce comes from the Canadian Rockies. Ultimately about 2m (6ft) tall, they are widely planted in gardens and rockeries. Alberta spruce are tough plants which can take full sun, but for the best foliage colour use dappled shade.

TRUNK

The habit is upright and tapered and the trees are often multi-trunked. The trunk form and branch periphery are very conical and the dark green needles are dense and small. The bark is brown and thickens with age.

SOIL

Alberta spruce like well-drained soil and a mix of 5 parts mixed sand, 3 parts composted peat and 2 parts leaf mould will suit them very well.

POTTING AND REPOTTING

Repot as buds swell in the spring. Do not leave this until the buds have split their casing and extended. Repot every three to four years, and less often as the tree ages. Do not repot in the autumn.

WATERING

Keep the trees damp but not soggy. After the needles have set their length and feel firm, mist the foliage.

FEEDING

Feed with Miracle-Gro at half strength every two weeks from bud swell until early summer. Do not feed from mid- to late summer. Feed with 0–10–10 once a month from early to mid-autumn.

TRIMMING

Pinch extending shoots when they are long enough to take with the soft part of thumb and forefinger, not the nails. If you go in any closer, you are pinching too deep and the shoot may well die. Watch the terminal shoots, as these quickly grow away and inner buds suffer as they are bypassed. It may take a while to prune the whole tree, as the buds open in a diffused way over an extended period. Occasional thinning will be necessary to open up the inside branches so that they can receive light and air. Often this means sacrificing some limbs so that the chosen ones can breathe and remain fully active. Branches are pruned in early autumn.

WIRING

Wire in autumn after branch pruning. Keep wired trees frost free.

PESTS

Red spider, woolly aphids and mealy bugs are the main pests - treat as for Scots pine.

DISEASES

Substantially free.

STYLING

Formal and group styles suit the structured growth habit of this tree.

YEW

Taxus species

HABITAT AND PLACEMENT

Yews are distributed throughout Europe, Algeria, North America, Canada and Japan. They are evergreen shrubs and trees that thrive in many environments and are tolerant of chalk soils, as well as shade - where they take on deep leaf colour.

TRUNK

The trunk becomes massive with age. It can become fissured, fluted and multi-trunked. The bark is dark red to brown and peels in strips with age.

SOIL

Although yews are very adaptable in open growth, once potted they seem to prefer a light, well-drained soil. A mixture of 5 parts mixed sand, 3 parts leaf mould and 2 parts composted bark or akadama is a good one to try.

POTTING AND REPOTTING

Repot every two to three years. The English yew (*Taxus baccata*) has very fine feeder roots that need careful handling. It seems contradictory that such a widely adapted plant should be root touchy, but it does seem that if you are heavy handed when you repot and use pressure so that the drainage slows down, the tree can be badly affected. Trim and even the roots in the usual way, then just lightly lay the soil in around the roots rather than firming it and the tree will be fine. The roots of other yew species are not so tricky. Repot in spring as the buds swell.

WATERING

Keep the trees damp, never soggy, as the fine roots rot easily. Misting the leaves is beneficial and dappled or deeper shade will help maintain moisture levels without the need for constant soil irrigation. The trees enjoy such conditions.

FEEDING

Feed every two weeks from early spring to early summer with half-strength Miracle-Gro. Feed again once a month from early to mid-autumn with 0–10–10. The fine roots will benefit from the ripening and hardening effects of this type of feed as they go into winter.

TRIMMING

Trim back soft new growth when it extends beyond 5cm (2in) or so. Heavier growth can be scissor cut. Well-fed and correctly watered plants will erupt inner buds after pruning. Thin out surplus buds. Groom by removing inner growth along the inner parts of the branches and their junctions with the trunk. Prune all ascending and descending shoots. Prune old branches in early autumn.

WIRING

Use aluminium wire, and wire in the autumn. Afterwards, keep the trees frost free. De-wire after a year, but watch for tightness and release the wire promptly if necessary.

PESTS

Scale insects are the main problem. Use malathion or Volck and scrub off the bodies to make sure you can distinguish any fresh attack.

DISEASES

Substantially free.

STYLING

All the styles except broom are suitable for yews.

glossary

akadama Japanese red subsoil.

aphids Greenfly.

broom style Bonsai style with upright trunk and branches like an inverted broom.

coral spot Fungus producing pinhead size salmon-pink pustules.

crackle glaze Glaze featuring a crazing of small superficial cracks.

cut-and-grow method Pruning technique where growth is stopped and forced to change direction.

Cut Wound Paste Japanese wound sealant.

deciduous Trees that shed their leaves in autumn.

dimethoate Systemic insecticide.

evergreen Trees that hold their leaves.

exfoliating Rough-textured bark that is peeling or curling off in layers or scales.

Fish Emulsion Mild fertilizer of around 5–2–2 to nourish growth.

formal Bonsai style in which the trunk is vertical and the branches radiate up the tree.

grid Mesh used to locate plants when creating a group planting.

group More than two trees in a planting.

ibigawa rock Japanese stone which is grey/black/white.

informal Upright bonsai style where the trunk is shaped in soft curves.

Kiyonal Japanese wound sealant.

Lac-Balsam German wound sealant

leaning Bonsai style in which the trunk leans off the vertical.

malathion Contact insecticide.

mealy bug White, waxy-coated insect pest.

Miracid High-nitrogen fertilizer for acid-loving plants.

Miracle-Gro Fertilizer for general use.

negative space Shapes created between the 'positives' of branch and trunk outlines.

0–10–10 Fertilizer with that analysis, good for flower and fruit production and for hardening off plants ready for winter.

pot-on soil Fresh soil placed around a previously pot-bound tree to invigorate it.

raft Bonsai style with a recumbent trunk and branches as trees.

red spider Minute, spider-like pest that makes webs.

root connected Bonsai style with root suckers as trunks connected through the roots.

saikei Japanese term for landscape plantings.

scale insect Pests with turtle-like shells.

soft pruning/soft pinching Taking off green growth with the fingers.

spur pruned Branches trimmed back adjacent to short, characterful side branches.

suiban Decorative pot without holes for display of rock plantings.

tap root Main anchor root.

taper Trunk form that gradually thins as it rises.

TEF Trace Element Frit, a powdered compound containing all the micronutrients needed for sound plant growth.

terminals Growth tips.

Volck Environmentally safe, emulsion spray insecticide.

yatsubusa Japanese term for trees with dwarf, compact growth.

zineb Fungicide used against needle cast.

index

accent plants 39, 47, 49, 57, 69
    use 37, 51
accessory plants 30, 31, 37
Acer see maple
aftercare
    landscapes 81, 89
    trees 114–125
ageing 58–60
akadama 38
American larch *see* larch
Anderson, Charlie and Ruth 10–17
aphids 42–43

bark texture 59
Barton, Dan 39, 47, 57, 69
Barton, Phyl 40, 49
beech (*Fagus*)
    European (*F. sylvatica*) 46
    Japanese White (*F. crenata*) 46
    tree care 114–115
bonsai nurseries 44–46
box (*Buxus*) 46
    B. sempervirens 'Kingsville' 18–19,
        100–101
    tree care 115
branches
    condition 45–46
    shaping 55–58, 60
broom style 13, 14–15, 63
Buxus see box

Carex 69
Carex see grasses
Carpinus see hornbeam
carving 59
'Catlin' elm *see* elm
cedar, Japanese (*Cryptomeria
    japonica*) 46–48
C.j. 'Tansu' 73–81
tree care 115–116
Chamaecyparis see cypress
Chinese elm *see* elm
Chinese juniper *see* juniper
ciment fondu 31, 83–87

clover, black (*Trifolium repens
    purpurescens*) 48
clump style 10–11, 92–93
combing, roots 54
containers 54
    choosing 38
    rock planter 84–87
Cotoneaster 48
    tree care 116–117
Cryptomeria see cedar
Cut Wound Paste 39
cypress, Sawara (*Chamaecyparis
    pisifera*) 48
    tree care 117–118

Derderian, Connie 18, 22
diseases 114–125
drainage 31, 54
Duffett, Gordon 15, 35

elm, Chinese (*Ulmus parvifolia*)
    12–13, 48, 94–95
    tree care 118–119
    U. p. 'Catlin' 29, 110–111
    U. p. 'Seiju' 14–15, 96–97
Enwright, Genieve and Jack 18–25
European hornbeam *see* hornbeam

Fagus spp. *see* beech
feeding 39, 60
    tree requirements 114–125
fertilizer 39, 60
Fish Emulsion 39
foliage, condition 41
formal style 61–62
Furakawa, Masahiro 8–9

garden centres 41–44
grasses 37, 51, 57, 69
groups 10–25, 29, 92–107, 110–111
    forming 66–68

habitats 114–125
hemlock (*Tsuga*)

Eastern (*T. canadensis*) 48
tree care 119
Western (*T. heterophylla*) 16–17,
    48, 98–99
hornbeam, European (*Carpinus
    betulus*) 48
    multi-trunk group 22–23,
        104–105
    tree care 119–120

ibigawa rock 8–9, 90–91
implied space 7
informal style 64–65
insect damage 42
insecticides 43
iris 40

Japanese maple *see* maple
Japanese red soil 38
juniper (*Juniperus*)
    Chinese (*J. chinensis*) 48–50
        J. c. 'San José' 30–31, 112
        raft style 8–9, 90–91
    Chinese (*J. × media*) 48–50
    tree care 120–121

'Kingsville' box *see* box
Kiyonal 39

Lac-Balsam 39
lakes 12–13, 94–95
landscapes
    American larch 24–25, 106–107
    'Catlin' elm 29, 110–111
    Chinese elm 12–13, 94–95
    Chinese juniper 8–9, 90–91
    European hornbeam 22–23,
        104–105
    Japanese maple 20–21, 102–103
    'Kingsville' box 18–19, 100–101
    'San José' juniper 30–31, 112
    'Seiju' elm 14–15, 96–97
    Trident maple 10–11, 32–35,
        92–93, 113

Western hemlock 16–17, 98–99
'Yatsubusa' Japanese maple
26–28, 108–109
larch (*Larix*)
American (*L. laricina*)24–25,
106–107
European (*L. decidua*) 50
Japanese (*L. kaempferi* syn. *L.
leptolepis*) 50
tree care 121–122
Larix see larch
layering 71, 108–109
leaf mould 38
leaning style 66
lime sulphur 60
location guide 67–68, 75–77

maintenance 60–61, 81
malathion 43
maple, Japanese (*Acer palmatum*) 50
A. p. 'Yatsubusa', root-connected
26–28, 108–109
group 20–21, 102–103
tree care 122
maple, Trident (*Acer buergerianum*)
50
clump style 10–11, 92–93
raft style 32–35, 113
tree care 122–123
materials
bonsai 38–39
rock planter 84
Miracid 39
Miracle-Gro 39
mondo grass (*Ophiopogon japonicus*
var. 'Nana' syn. *O. j.* 'Kyoto
Dwarf') 30
moss 79, 81

nurseries 44–46

0-10-10 39
Ophiopogon japonicus see mondo
grass

Pacific Rim Bonsai Collection
29–31
Patterson, Tim 12, 16
peat 38
perspective 7
pests 114–125
Phalaris 57

Phalaris see grasses
Picea see spruce
pine, Scots (*Pinus sylvestris*) 50
tree care 123–124
placement 60–61, 114–125
planting 67–68, 73–81
plants, choosing 37, 41–51
potentilla 47
preparation, landscape plants
74–75
projects
landscapes 73–81, 90–113
rock planter 83–87
pruning
maintenance 81
roots 53–55, 75
trunks and branches 56

raft style 8–9, 32–33, 70, 90–91,
113
red spider 42
repotting 114–125
Rhododendron serpyllifolium 31
rivers 18–19, 30–31, 101, 112
rock planter 84–87
rocks 7, 38
ibigawa 8–9, 90–91
landscapes 8–9, 16–17, 90–91,
98–99
rockspray *see Cotoneaster*
root-connected trees 26–28, 71,
108–109
roots
condition 43–44, 45
pruning 53–55, 75
surface 59, 62, 63

saikei 12–13, 30–31, 94–95, 112
'San José' juniper *see* juniper
sand 38
scale insects 42
'Seiju' elm *see* elm
shaping
plants 53–71
rock planter 84
sieves 38
silvering 60
Sisyrinchium 39
soil 38, 55, 76–77
plant purchases 46
tree requirements 114–125
space 7

spruce, Alberta (*Picea* var. *glauca
albertiana*) 50
tree care 124–125
stone 38
styling 61–71
tree species 114–125
Susuki, Harvey 10

taper, trunk shape 56, 59
Taxus see yew
texture 7, 44
tools 38–39
Trace Element Frit 39
trees
see also landscapes
care 114–125
choosing 41–46
descriptions 46–51
Trident maple *see* maple, Trident
Trifolium see clover
trimming 114–125
trunk
angle 58–59
condition 44–45
shaping 55–58
tree characteristics 114–125
Tsuga see hemlock
Tucker, Melba 29

Ulmus see elm

Volck 43

water effect 38
lake 12–13, 94–95
river 18–19, 30–31, 101, 112
watering 60
tree requirements 114–125
Western hemlock *see* hemlock
wiring 55–58, 62–66, 114–125
wound sealant 39

'Yatsubusa' Japanese maple *see*
maple, Japanese
yew (*Taxus baccata*) 50–51
tree care 125
Yoneda, Kaz 30
Young, Carl and Shin 14